How To Manage Anger
Gaining Control Of Ourselves

*A Complete Guide To
Anger Management*

GEORGE ANDERSON, LCSW, BCD
PUBLISHED BY ANDERSON & ANDERSON, A.P.C.
http://www.AndersonServices.com

Copyright © 1997 George Anderson.
Revised, December 2005.

ISBN: 0-9743682-3-7

V2.20040918

Printed by Image Square Print & Graphics. All rights reserved. Athough the author has made every effort to ensure the accuracy and completeness of information contained in this book, we assume no responsibility for errors, inaccuracies, omissions, or any inconsistency herein. Any slight of people, places, or organizations is unintentional. May not be reproduced in whole or in part in any form or by any means.

About George Anderson

George Anderson is a Board Certified Diplomate in Psychotherapy, A Fellow in the American Orthopsychiatric Association and, the first global provider of Anger Management training, workbooks, videos, DVDs and interactive CDs. He is the author of "Gaining Control of Ourselves", "Controlling Ourselves", "Parenting in A Troubled World", "The California Domestic Violence Intervention Curriculum", and "Depression, Awareness, Recognition and Intervention".

Mr. Anderson received Post Graduate training in Child and Adolescent Psychotherapy from the Harvard University School of Medicine (1971) and previously taught in the UCLA Neuropsychiatric Institute, Pepperdine University, and Simmons College School of Social Work. Currently, he is the major provider of language and culture specific curricula in Anger Management, Executive Coaching for physicians and Domestic Violence Intervention. His workbooks are published in English, Vietnamese, Korean, Italian, Canadian French, Spanish and Russian.

George Anderson was the technical consultant on the popular Jack Nicholson/Adam Sandler Movie "Anger Management". He also appeared on the Cover of the Los Angeles Times Magazine in its August 28, 2005 edition titled "The Least Angry Man". This article is listed on our website as "The Storm's Quiet Eye" at Anderson & Anderson Online Resources. A sitcom on his anger management practice is currently in the works.

Gaining Control of Ourselves

Table of Contents

Table of Contents i
Acknowledgements iv
Foreward v
Preface vi
Goals vii
   Group Objectives: vii
   Group Responsibilities: vii
   Group Rules viii
Part 1: Gaining Better Control and Understanding of Ourselves 1
   Control Log 3
   Constructive Interactions (Positive Wheel) 4
   Destructive Interactions (Negative Wheel) 5
   Positive Wheel Definitions 6
   Negative Wheel Definitions 7
   Sample Control Log Entries 8
      Anger: What Is It? What Causes It? 16
         Anger is learned 16
      Anger Checklist – How Is Your Anger? 17
      The Heavy Costs of Anger 18
         Why change? 19
         Anger Destroys Personal Relationships 19
         Let it go 20
         Anger Destroys School and Work Relationships 20
         Anger pushes people away 20
         Be in control 20
         Anger – the energy magnet 21
         Perception is reality 21
         Anger Makes Bad Situations Worse 21
         Things work well when you are not angry 22
         Anger is not a universal tool 22
         Anger Often Leads To Aggression 22
   Personal/Self-Awareness Inventory 24
      Section 1 24
      Section 2 25
      Section 3 27
      Section 4 28
      Section 5 30
      Section 6 32
   Part 2: Stress Management 36
      Some stress is normal 36
      Is it worth dying for? 36
      One Step at a time 36
      You have a choice 37

Gaining Control of Ourselves

What Is Stress?	37
Stress is Mental	37
Stress May Be Beneficial	38
Stress May Be Harmful	38
Three Skills for Managing Stress	38
Skill 1: Awareness	39
Identifying Your Stressors	39
Recognizing your stress symptoms	40
Skill 2: Acceptance	44
Keep Situations in Perspective	44
Use Self-Dialogue	45
Keep a Positive Attitude	45
Develop a "Stress-Resistant" Personality	46
Get Counseling	47
Skill 3: Coping Skills	47
Just Do It!	48
Relaxation	48
Get away from it all	49
Reflect On What We Have Learned	50
Another Way of Managing Stress:	52
Systematic Desensitization	52
How Well Do You Manage Stress?	53
Acceptance Skill Questions	54
Coping Skill Questions	54
Action Skill Questions	54
Communication Skill Questions	54
Become A Better Listener	55
Stress Log	57
Strategies to Handle High-Risk Situations	59
Review: Stress Test	60
Part 3: Emotional Intelligence	62
Develop an Understanding of Yourself	64
Recognize Patterns of Behavior	65
Learn to Think of Consequences	66
Ask for and Listen to Advice	67
Motivation is Key to Change	69
Increase Empathy	69
Managing Negative Emotions	70
General Guidelines	70
Depression	72
Anger	75
Anger as a Response to Fear	77
Responding to and Learning from Anger	77
Some Reasons For Anger	79
Some Reasons To Give Up Anger	80
Recognizing Anger	80

- Identifying High-Risk Situations 84
- Negative Feelings, Attitudes, Thoughts, or Behaviors: 84
  - Problems in Relationships with Other People 85
  - Other High-Risk Situations 86
- The Anger Log 87
  - Step 1: 91
  - Step 2: 94
- Seven Steps to Anger Control 96
- Taking a Time-Out 97
  - Steps to Take: 97
  - Why Does a Time-Out Work? 98
  - Time-Outs Are Hard To Do! 99
- Strategies to Handle High-Risk Situations 100
- Review 102
- Part 4: Communication 104
  - Improving Communication with Others 104
  - Self–Assessment: 105
  - Understanding and Dealing with Feelings 105
  - Roadblocks to Open Communication 107
    - Phrases for Miscommunication 108
  - Positive Communication Skills 109
    - Silence, Passive Listening: 109
    - Simple Acknowledgement: 109
    - Door Openers: 109
    - Active Listening: 110
    - Examples of some Active Listening Responses 110
    - Phrases For Active Listening 111
  - Styles of Communication 112
    - "I" Messages: Taking Responsibility for What You Feel 113
    - Guidelines to Resolving Conflicts with Intimate Partners 114
  - What Is Open For Negotiation In Intimate Relationships? 116
  - Remember These Four Points About Respectful Communication and Conflict Resolution .. 118
  - Quiz: 119
    - Improving Communication 119
  - Action Plan 120
- Part 5: Role Modeling 122
  - Communication by Example 122
  - Quiz 124
- Appendix 126
- Selected Bibliography 127
  - Anger 127
  - Stress 127
  - Emotional Intelligence 128
  - Communication 129
- Index 131

Acknowledgements

I want to thank Angela Liu for her many in-depth discussions and constructive comments. Much of the work that went into the completion of this manuscript can be credited to her. She worked diligently to refine the material and present it in legible form. I sincerely appreciate her efforts.

My sister and friend, Alfreda Scott, read the manuscript and offered invaluable advice to improve its user-friendliness. She gently persuaded us to keep the material simple in order to reach the general population of persons most likely to attend an Anger Management class.

This revised version of the original book has an additional section on Emotional Intelligence which proved popular when field-tested in anger management groups offered in our Brentwood office. Mr. Howard Kim, M.A., M.Th., is responsible for translating this manuscript into Korean. He also contributed to the development of the Contrasting Wheels of Behavior which are used as anchors to this revised edition. These Wheels assist the reader in providing a quick reference to positive and negative behaviors that either enhance or inhibit healthy interactions with others. John Elder, M.A., has tirelessly edited the manuscript.

My wife Nancy, daughter Ania, and sons Bryan and Jason, provided me with a supportive environment and an opportunity to practice the positive skills presented in this workbook.

GEORGE ANDERSON, Brentwood, California
July, 2002

Foreward

In 1997, Anderson & Anderson published the first edition of this workbook. I was introduced to this publication while serving as Acting Dean of the Charles R. Drew School of Medicine, College of Allied Health Sciences. George Anderson served as one of our Curriculum Consultants with special emphasis on our violence prevention curricula.

We were impressed with the way Mr. Anderson was able to translate complex material regarding anger management that captures the attention of the reader while teaching concrete skills to manage stress and anger. The workbook also incorporates content and exercises to simultaneously improve communication and increase emotional intelligence.

The 1997 edition far exceeded all expectations. It has been published in English, Spanish, and Korean and is currently in use in nearly ninety jails and prisons, five public school districts, and hundreds of after-school programs throughout the nation. The College of Allied Health Sciences is the first public health program to offer the Anderson & Anderson anger management and batterers' intervention curricula as areas of specialization in public health.

It is difficult to believe, but this current edition is even more impressive than the one it replaces. The most dramatic change is the inclusion of two Contrasting Wheels of Interactions. These two wheels are the anchors to this new edition of the workbook. They can and should be referred to when completing exercises on anger, stress, communication or emotional intelligence. These wheels demonstrate in simple, easy-to-understand terms what to avoid in relating to others and which skills are important to practice for improving interpersonal relationships. The Destructive Interaction or Negative Wheel helps to remind the participant what not to do, while the Constructive Interaction Wheel offers eight spokes designed to be used in increasing emotional intelligence and positive interpersonal relationships. I highly endorse this publication.

Dr. Roosevelt Jacobs, Acting Dean
Charles R. Drew School of Medicine, College of Allied Health Sciences
Los Angeles, California

Preface

This workbook is designed to be used by persons who have problems managing angry feelings. It can be used as a self-help book, as a resource for groups, and for anger management programs mandated by the probation department, human resource departments, or the courts. The Anderson & Anderson workbook is currently being used by the Los Angeles District of the United States Postal Service in its Employee Assistance Program to reduce interpersonal conflict as well as the Los Angeles Airport Police Department. A number of Colleges and Universities have adopted it for use with students referred for disciplinary infractions by the Deans of Student Services. A partial list of Colleges and Universities using this workbook includes the University of Southern California, Charles Drew School of Medicine, School of Allied Health Sciences, Pierce College, Los Angeles Harbor College, Long Beach College and West Los Angeles Junior College. It is used in school districts in Sacramento, Centinella, Santa Clarita, Los Angeles and Compton, California.

The simplicity and presentation of the material in this workbook has resulted in its selection as the model for use in a Sony Pictures Jack Nicholson/Adam Sandler movie entitled *Anger Management*, on which George Anderson was the technical consultant.

Anger is a basic human emotion. It is used to express negative feelings such as fear, rage, unhappiness, discontent, depression, etc. We may have observed that individuals often gain attention, control, and influence when they get angry. We can say that our expression of anger is a learned response; therefore, we can unlearn those behaviors and "recondition" ourselves.

The primary goal of this workbook is to teach acceptable expressions of anger and to eliminate violent and self-destructive behaviors in our lives. You will learn to identify and control your own anger so that it does not become a destructive force. Like learning any new skill, practice is necessary to incorporate the techniques offered.

Learning is not attained by chance. It must be sought for with ardor and attended to with diligence
-- Abigail Adams

Goals

This program is designed to help individuals recognize and manage anger. One of its goals is to teach acceptable ways of expressing anger. By gaining a better understanding of self, we will learn to better control our anger so that it does not lead to violent outbursts or actions that are harmful to others. Also, we will learn different techniques for stress management and enhancing emotional intelligence. Lastly, we will devote lessons to improving communications so that we may become better listeners and communicators to prevent angry situations. Participants are encouraged to complete all of the exercises in the book and practice applying the techniques in real-life situations.

Group Objectives:

At the end of this course, participants will be able to:
- Recognize the role of individual responsibility in changing "maladaptive" behavior.
- Develop a working understanding of one's own anger/stress patterns and responses.
- Identify "situational anger" that consistently results in angry responses that can lead to violent behavior.
- Eliminate or minimize violent behavior. Learn how and when to use "time-outs" to prevent violent confrontations. Incorporate new coping skills to handle anger, stress, and other feelings.
- Use communication skills and listening techniques effectively and gain a better understanding of how children in one's family can be affected by parental communication techniques.
- Become more aware of one's own stress and anger signals and develop the capacity to sense the mood of persons with whom he or she must interact.

Group Responsibilities:

- Keep a daily Anger Log and Stress Journal.
- Identify anger and stressful situations.
- Identify your own anger and stress cues (become aware of how you feel when you are feeling angry or stressed and how you behave when you are feeling this way).
- Implement the skills learned so that you can gain better control of yourself.
- Master the eight spokes on each of our two Contrasting Wheels of Behavior.

Gaining Control of Ourselves

Group Rules

1. Participants must come on time to all classes
2. Fees must be paid prior to each class and must be kept current.
3. No participant will be permitted to complete the class until all outstanding fees are paid in full.
4. No profanity will be permitted in the class.
5. The identity of all participants as well as any material discussed in the group will be kept confidential.
6. Participants who are disruptive in the group will be reported back to the court or referring source as uncooperative.
7. All group members must participate in each class.
8. Homework assignments are expected to be completed.
9. Any participant who appears to be under the influence of drugs or alcohol will be dismissed from the group and reported back to court or referring source.
10. No derogatory, racial, or ethnic comments will be accepted in the group.
11. Group time will not be used to answer questions regarding any member's account balance or number of remaining sessions.
12. All cell phones or pagers must be turned off during class time.
13. Consistent attendance is required.

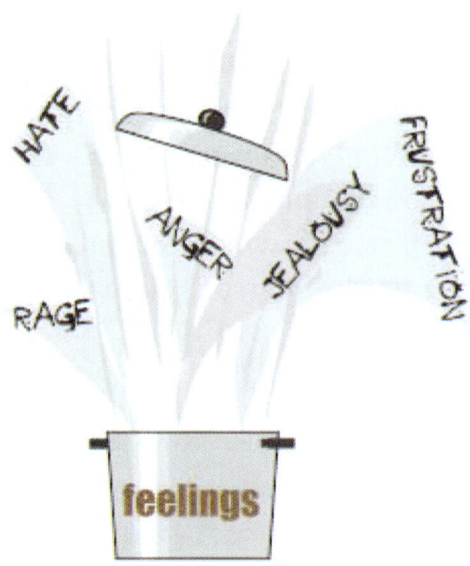

Part 1: Gaining Better Control and Understanding of Ourselves

Stress and anger have been identified as two principal factors that tend to occur in an act of aggression toward another person. We believe that participants can be taught to recognize and manage these two important contributing factors, which are roadblocks to positive healthy interpersonal relationships.

Unrecognized or untreated stress tends to lead to frustration, anger, and – all too often – aggressive outbursts: road rage and desk rage are two examples. Again, stress and anger are not the problem, **person-directed aggression** is the behavior that must be stopped.

This book will focus on four basic areas: **C**ommunication, **A**nger Management, **S**tress Management, and **E**motional Intelligence. An easy way to remember these four key subjects is to use the acronym **CASE**.

<u>C</u>ommunication is Important

We also believe communication is essential to improving relations with others. This area is often problematic in relationships with persons who have explosive personalities. The latter part of this workbook introduces some key mechanisms for "improving" communications with others.

<u>A</u>nger is a Primitive Emotion

Anger is a feeling of displeasure, which usually shows itself in a desire to fight back at the supposed cause. It is accompanied by physical changes in the body. When we are angry, our pulse may become more rapid, our blood pressure may rise, adrenaline will enter the bloodstream, and muscles may become tense. The combination of angry feelings and physical arousal often propel people into action. All too often, people act out violently or aggressively as a result of their anger. Hence, in anger management sessions, we encourage each participant to talk about his or her angry feelings rather than to act upon them.

<u>S</u>tress is a Step toward Anger

The second issue of focus in this book is stress. We encounter numerous stressors in our daily lives. Stress is our body's natural response to the physical and emotional pressures of life. A moderate amount of stress can help us perform at our peak level. Too much stress, however, makes us ineffective, troubled, and even sick. Because of these negative consequences, we have devoted several lessons to stress management.

Gaining Control of Ourselves

Emotional Intelligence
Not understanding or recognizing your own inner feelings is frequently a factor in aggressive or violent outbursts. The personal inventory questionnaire and the lessons in this text are designed to help each participant gain a better understanding of him/herself by examining a wide range of responses to questions designed to assist the participant in taking an inventory of him/herself. Understanding our weaknesses as well as our strengths is an important factor in emotional intelligence. We believe strongly in the importance of increasing the emotional intelligence of all participants.

> Anyone can become angry--that is easy. But to be angry with the right person, to the right degree, at the right time, for the right purpose, and in the right way--this is not easy.
>
> -- Aristotle

Gaining Control of Ourselves

Control Log

DATE ____ / ____ / ____

***ACTIONS*:**
Briefly describe the incident that resulted in your referral to this program.

1. What did you want to happen in this situation?

2. What caused you to think that your actions would get the results you wanted?

3. What feelings were you having?

4. Did you attempt to make light of your role in this situation? Did you attempt to blame the victim?

5. What was the impact of your action?
   - On you:

   - On the victim:

   - On others:

6. Did any past violence or aggression on your part affect this situation?

7. What could you have done differently?

Gaining Control of Ourselves

Constructive Interactions
(Positive Wheel)

The Wheels, which appear below, are the anchors to this anger management workbook. They can and should be referred to when focusing on or practicing positive skills of interaction. They are also a quick reference for recognizing styles of speaking, aggressive behavior and habit patterns, which make healthy relationships difficult. Tools for increasing emotional intelligence must be incorporated in mastering the spokes on the Positive Wheel.

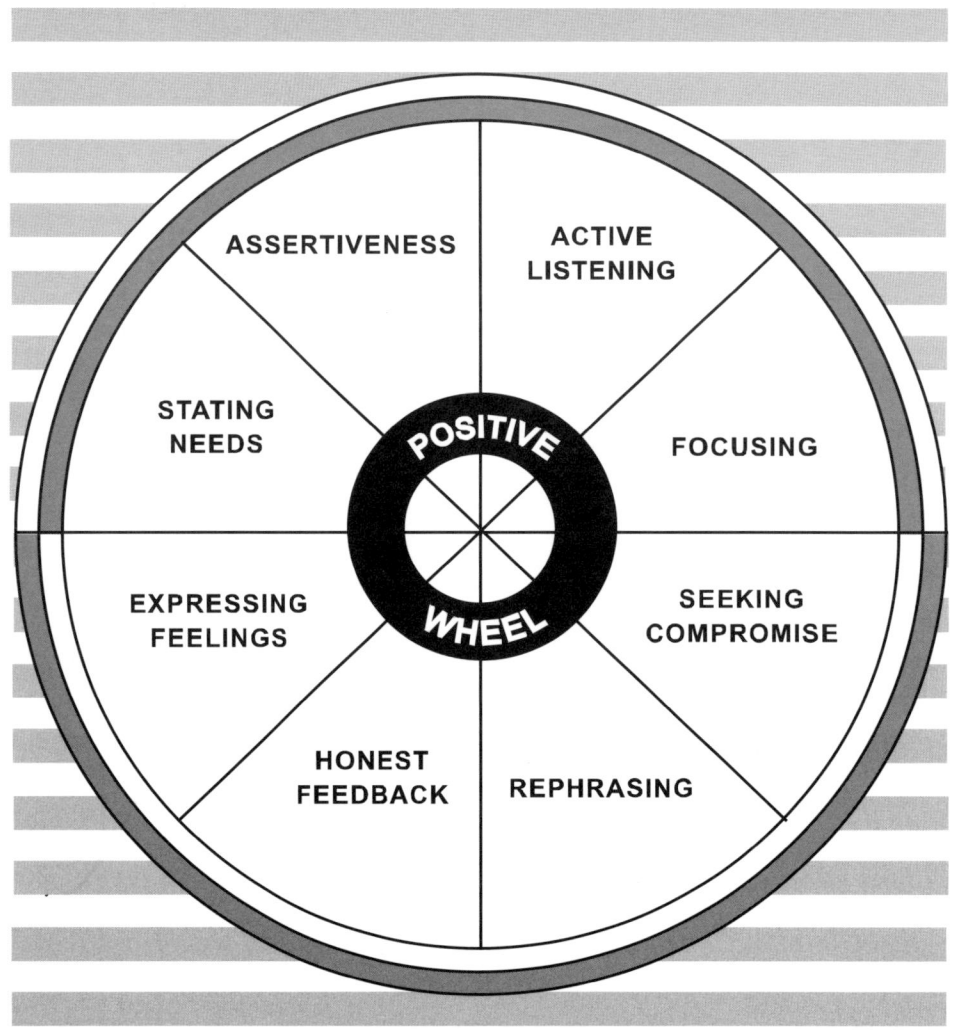

Anderson & Anderson

Destructive Interactions
(Negative Wheel)

This Negative Wheel helps link the different behaviors that together form a pattern of miscommunication. It shows the relationship as a whole – and how each seemingly unrelated behavior is an important part in an overall effort to dominate a situation or someone else.

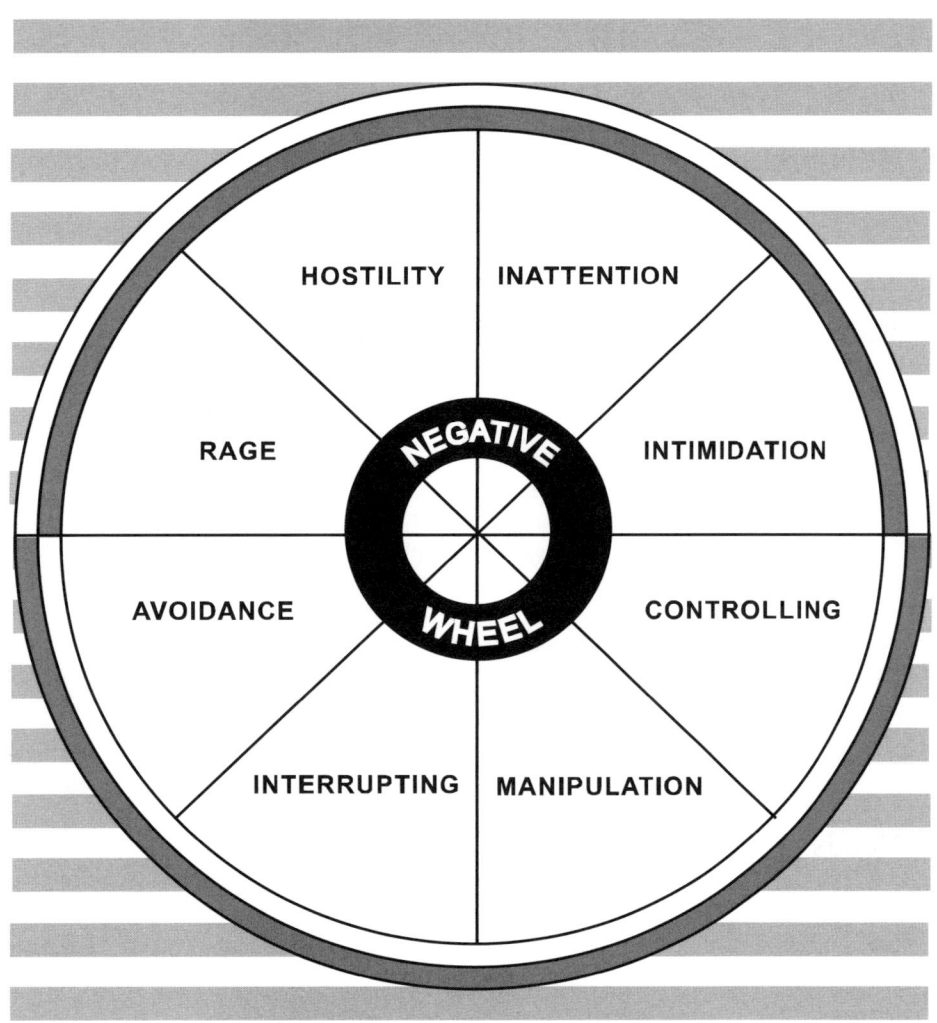

Gaining Control of Ourselves

Positive Wheel Definitions

Define these terms in your own words:

Active Listening:

Focusing:

Seeking Compromise:

Rephrasing:

Honest Feedback:

Expressing Feelings:

Stating Needs:

Assertiveness:

ining Control of Ourselves

ative Wheel Definitions

r own words:

GIVE YOUR OPINION OF GROUP

Name: _____

Date of Group _____

Time of Group _____

Title of Group _____

Facilitator of Group _____

What did you learn from the topic? _____

What was your mood during group? _____

Hostility:

Sample Control Log Entries

The case vignettes below provide an excellent way to master the spokes on the Contrasting Wheels of Behavior. Practice in relating these stories to the spokes on the wheels will serve to help you recognize when you are exhibiting any of the behaviors that are impediments to positive interpersonal relationships. Further, it will help you to make the spokes on the Positive Wheel a regular part of your behavior.

Example 1

Situation: "I drive 40 miles each way to work on the worst freeway in the state (405). My job is very stressful. I have been stressed out a lot over the last two years. One night, I became angry with my daughter and smashed the monitor of her computer. My wife panicked and demanded that I go for anger management."

Beliefs: "I simply can't justify my actions. I am just stressed to the max."

Feelings: "I don't even think the issue was my daughter. I was frustrated over the bind that I am in. I have a high income, I don't want to move and I hate the drive."

Cost: "Respect for myself."

Past Violence: "None"

Alternatives: "I should have told my daughter that I was in a bad mood and I need her to do what I asked."

Gaining Control of Ourselves

Example 2

Situation: "I was waiting for a parking space in a shopping mall. Another car drove in and took my space. I displayed my service revolver. He called the police on his cell phone and I was arrested."

Beliefs: "The other driver was wrong and that's that."

Feelings: "I was outraged."

Cost of Anger: "I was placed on probation from my job as an immigration officer and I have to attend 26 sessions here in anger management."

Past violence: "None."

Alternatives: "Called the police myself"

Example 3

Situation: "I was at my doctor's office. There was a women talking on a cell phone while blocking me. I waited patiently and she failed to move. Finally, I got out my car and knocked on her window. She continued to talk on her phone while waving me away. I smashed her window."

Beliefs: "Naturally, I wanted her to move so that I could leave."

Feelings: "Angry"

Cost: "I am 72 years old and I find this class great. However, I am embarrassed the way I got here."

Past violence: "None."

Alternative: "I could have tried calling the police."

Gaining Control of Ourselves

Example 4

Situation: "A woman at my job had been repeatedly parking in my assigned space. I talked to her twice and left notes on her car window. She continued to park in my stall. Finally, I wrote her a threatening note and left it on her window."

Beliefs: "I wanted her to stop parking in my stall."

Feelings: "Really angry."

Cost: "The Partners of the firm demanded me to come here."

Past violence: "None."

Alternative: "I should have reported it to the Partners."

Example 5

Situation: "I have a hearing defect. You can see that I wear a hearing aid. I am Russian and I don't speak English well. It sometimes takes time for me to understand people when they speak to me if I can see their face. I have dinner and drinks at the same bar/restaurant most days. I am friendly with one waitress. One night I brought her flowers for her birthday and her boyfriend was there. He tried to say something to me and I did not understand him. He hit me and I threw a wine glass at him which cut his face."

Beliefs: "It is clear that this man did not understand my intentions."

Feelings: "Angry and confused"

Cost: "I was ordered to anger management and decided to take an online class. When I went back to court the Judge refused to give me credit and sent me here to start all over. I like the class and will recommend it to my daughter who is a teenager."

Past violence: "None."

Gaining Control of Ourselves

Example 6

Situation: "I was in a bar and got in a fight with another guy. I broke his jaw and was ordered to pay his medical bill, and complete 52 sessions of anger management. My job has been supportive and I am actually glad to be here."

Beliefs: "I was provoked by another guy who seemed to have been looking for a fight."

Feelings: "So angry I saw red"

Cost: "I am glad about the class but embarrassed about my actions. I am a religious person as is my family. No one in my family has even been arrested before."

Past violence: "None"

Example 7

Situation: "My boyfriend and I were at a club. The security guard got into an argument with my boy friend and he threw us out and began beating up on my boyfriend. I was wearing heels, so I spiked the guard with my shoes. It turned out that he was an off duty police officer who arrested me. I was given anger management. "

Beliefs: "I thought the Officers action was wrong. He seemed too impressed with his power."

Feeling: "I was furious."

Cost: "I got arrested. Had to hire a lawyer and attend this class."

Past violence: "None."

Gaining Control of Ourselves

Example 8

Situation: "I had a party at my home. My next door neighbor came over and complained about the noise. We had an argument. He called the police and they came and disrespected me in my own home. One officer claimed that I was resisting arrest so I was arrested and charged with resisting arrest. I was sent to anger management for 52 weeks."

Beliefs: "The Police overreacted. It was my house and my party. I was disrespected and roughed up."

Cost: "I was ordered to take this class, complete community services and pay a fine."

Past violence: "Most Black men here in L.A. will ultimately have problems with the police."

Alternatives: "Probably none."

Example 9

Situation: "My girlfriend and I broke up. I found out that she was going out with another guy. I went to her house and I smashed the window of the guy's car. It was the wrong car. I later found the right guy and smashed his window and I was arrested, went to court and got 26 weeks and probation."

Beliefs: "I thought this guy should have not been hitting on my lady."

Feelings: "I was mad as hell."

Cost: "I have to drive two hours to get here for these classes and my mother has to pay. I also had to pay for both car windows."

Past Violence: "Yes, I have been on probation before."

Alternative: "I don't know."

Gaining Control of Ourselves

Example 10

Situation: "I am here voluntarily; I have a 19 year old son. We bought him a car for his high school graduation. I asked him three times over two weeks to have the oil changed and I gave him the money to have it done. Finally, I became anger and told him that I felt like killing him. My wife felt that my response was too extreme and asked that I go for anger management."

Beliefs: "Since we bought my son the car which he wanted and we pay all of the cost, I thought it was reasonable for him to at least take it to have the oil changed."

Feelings: "First I was angry and immediately I felt really bad and ashamed of myself. My wife could not believe it."

Cost: "I don't see it as a cost. I need this."

Past violence: "Never."

Alternatives: "I should have tried to reason with him and involve his mom."

Example 11

Situation: "I was jaywalking in downtown Los Angeles and a Policeman tried to give me a ticket and I threw a coke in his face."

Beliefs: "I wanted him to focus on more important crime and leave me alone."

Feelings: "I felt pissed to the max. I was so angry, I couldn't think straight. Jay walking is no big deal."

Cost: "I lost my license as a Registered Nurse. I lost my job. I was placed in Jail for four months and I have to attend 52 weeks of anger management."

Past Violence: "I have been surrounded by violence all of my life. My father was an abusive alcoholic. My family was dysfunctional and I had three bad marriages."

Alternatives: "Nothing."

Gaining Control of Ourselves

Example 12

Situation: "I was the manager at a movie theater which was sold to a group which did not favor women in management positions. I was harassed by the new owners. I felt that they were trying to force me to resign. One night I became angry and at the end of my shirt, I took all of the money from the receipts during my shift and gave it to a group of homeless people."

Beliefs: "There is no question about it. I was being discriminated against because I am female."

Feeling: "I felt angry and I still feel angry."

Cost: "I got arrested, probation, community service as well as this class."

Past Violence: "None."

Alternatives: "I should have filled a formal complaint with the Department of Labor."

Example 13

Situation: "My girlfriend and I broke up. I was angry and made some calls to her home. She recorded the calls and I was arrested for terrorist threats and sent here for anger management."

Beliefs: "I thought I could get me girl friend to change her mind."

Feelings: "I felt depressed and angry."

Past Violence: "None."

Alternatives: "I should have given up."

Gaining Control of Ourselves

Example 14

Situation: "I am an attorney. I work for the government. I am also an artist. I drew a picture about people jumping out of a high rise building and one of my colleagues thought that it was making light of 9/11 so she filed a complaint and I was shafted. I don't have problems with anger but I am a practical joker and I guess people don't like it."

Beliefs: "This was just a joke that went bad."

Feelings: "I did not have any particular feelings."

Past Violence: "Absolutely not."

Alternatives: "Not play practical jokes at work."

Anger: What Is It? What Causes It?

Anger is one of the most misunderstood and overused of human emotions. Anger is a reaction to an inner emotion and not a planned action. Anger is *energy*. It serves a purpose by giving people the drive and determination to cope with difficult situations. Anger is a *signal*. It tells us something about ourselves, other people, and the situations in which we find ourselves. Anger helps discharge tension. If handled well, *anger can help resolve conflict and improve relationships with others*. Anger is an easy emotion to show: everyone gets angry.

Anger is learned

The feelings underlying the anger reaction make us feel vulnerable and weak; anger makes us feel, at least momentarily, strong and in control. Our responses to anger are generally learned from our families during childhood. It is important to remember that *any learned behavior can be unlearned*. New skills can be learned as well as alternatives to the inappropriate expressions of anger in an anger management program. In addition, new skills for enhancing communication and managing stress can be gained.

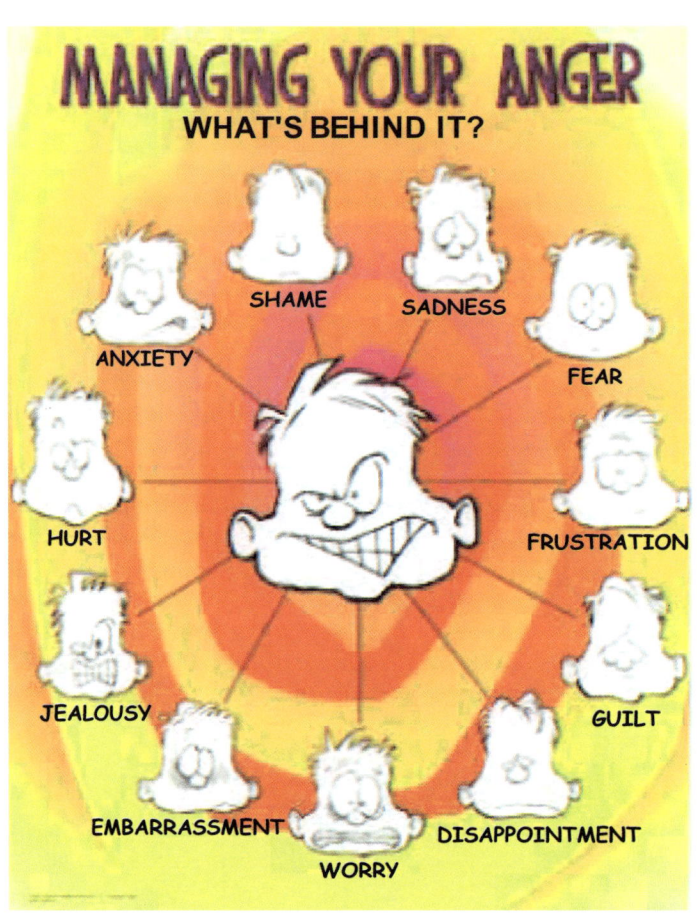

Gaining Control of Ourselves

Anger Checklist – How Is Your Anger?

This simple checklist will give you clues as to your handling of anger. Check a box for each one that applies to you.

- ❏ People tell you that you need to calm down.
- ❏ You feel tense much of the time.
- ❏ At work or school, you find yourself not saying what is on your mind.
- ❏ When you are upset, you try to block the world out by watching TV, reading a book or magazine, or going to sleep.
- ❏ You are drinking or smoking frequently to help you calm down.
- ❏ You have trouble going to sleep.
- ❏ You feel misunderstood or not listened too much of the time.
- ❏ People ask you not to yell or curse so much.
- ❏ Your loved ones keep saying that you are hurting them.
- ❏ Friends do not seek you out as much.

Scoring:

0-2 = MANAGEABLE: You may benefit from anger management training.
3-5 = MODERATE: You need to learn more about what stresses you out, and develop stress management and emotional intelligence techniques.
6+ = OUT OF CONTROL: You have an anger problem and could benefit from learning anger management techniques. You would benefit from an anger management class.

A careful review of this scoring indicates that *nearly everybody* can benefit from anger management.

The Heavy Costs of Anger

You are probably reading this book because either you or someone you care about has a problem with anger. Or, you may be a student attending this class as part of a violence prevention program for your school. Ideally, you have decided on your own that you can benefit from an anger management class and have enrolled in an effort to improve your ability to manage your anger. Before exploring how to reduce anger, let us take a look at some of the prices we pay for anger.

At one time or another, everyone experiences needless anger. Here are five specific signals that will tell you when your anger is creating problems for you.

1. *When it is too frequent.*
   There are many situations for which becoming angry is justified and natural. But, we often get angry when it is not necessary or useful. It is important to distinguish between the times when it is alright to be angry and when getting angry isn't a wise idea.

2. *When it is too intense.*
   Anger is something that occurs at different levels of intensity. A small or moderate amount of anger can often work to your advantage. High degrees of anger rarely produce positive results, and may damage your own physical health.

3. *When it lasts too long.*
   When anger continues over time, you maintain a level of arousal or stress that goes beyond normal limits. When anger does not go away, your body's systems are prevented from returning to normal levels, which makes it easier to get angry the next time something goes wrong. Sometimes, it becomes impossible to resolve.

4. *When it leads to aggression.*
   Aggressive acts are likely to result in trouble for you. When you feel you have been abused or treated unfairly, you may want to hurt the person who has offended you. Verbal aggression, like calling someone a name, is not helpful and often leads to a cycle of increasing aggression.

5. *When it destroys work or personal relationships.*
   When your anger interferes with doing a good job or makes it hard for people to relate to you, then it becomes a problem.

Why change?

Why should you and those you care about work to control your outbursts of anger or rage? Clearly, there is no law that says you must do so. But there are some important reasons why you may determine that it is in your best interest and helpful to those with whom you wish to relate.

Anger Destroys Personal Relationships

Damage to personal relationships is one of the most common costs of anger, and probably the worst. The relationships that are damaged are often your best. You may believe, like many people do, that anger is something we direct mostly at people we dislike. Unfortunately, we commonly make ourselves angry with persons we know well. The most frequent targets of anger include spouses, children, co-workers, and friends. Often, actions taken under intense anger are regretted after the damage is done.

Things to think about:
- Has your anger damaged any important relationships?
- Do you tend to blame people for how you are feeling?
- If you continue this pattern, where will you be a few years from now?

Gaining Control of Ourselves

Let it go

Letting go of your anger and being more accepting and flexible in close relationships will probably serve you better both long-term and short-term.

Anger Destroys School and Work Relationships

Let's face it, school and work are often very frustrating. Demanding teachers, parents, supervisors, jealous co-workers, irate customers, deadlines, and unfairness of all sorts – these can all test your patience. Your anger about frustrations, however, can frustrate you even more. Anger can ruin school and work relationships and limit your success. It can also block your ability to focus on important issues, perform quality work, and earn good grades.

Anger pushes people away

Getting along with other people helps you succeed at school or on the job and may even be as important as your ability to do the job itself. Teachers, co-workers and supervisors will hate working with you if you have temper outbursts. They will see you as a difficult person and go all-out to avoid contact or interaction with you. A study conducted by the Center for Creative Leadership in North Carolina found that, among executives, the inability to handle anger, especially in pressure situations, was a major factor in missing promotions, being fired, or being asked to retire. In a school setting, the students who earn the best grades are usually the ones who also are successful in getting along well with teachers and other students.

Be in control

Being able to manage your emotions on the job or at school, in spite of the usual frustrations, is often crucial in building a successful work or school career. Venting your anger often feels great to you – but not necessarily to your classmates or associates. Currently, a new term – "desk rage" – is being used to describe inappropriate displays of aggression at work. And, school violence is a concern for students and adults throughout the nation.

Gaining Control of Ourselves

Anger – the energy magnet

Anger also diverts your energy and attention away from your work. Instead, there is the tendency to focus on revenge, to plot against the other person or even to try to sabotage someone else's work. Those around you will likely notice your rage over time.

Perception is reality

It is likely that you will find yourself in work or classroom situations that are unfair and not rewarding. But by reacting angrily or impulsively, you encourage people to believe that you cannot handle frustration and are likely to explode in rage when things get tough. A much better alternative is to reduce your anger and do your best to improve the situation. If this does not work, you may calmly and rationally decide to seek help from someone who may assist you in seeking alternatives. Or you may request a transfer to a more rewarding environment. Ideally, you will seek out an anger management program to assist you in learning skills to manage anger and improve interpersonal relationships.

Anger Makes Bad Situations Worse

In spite of what we have just said, doesn't anger have some positives? Doesn't feeling angry sometimes help you face difficult situations? Won't it help you to feel empowered and in control when confronted with adversity? Isn't expressing your anger necessary for asserting yourself and getting your point across? These are all good questions. Many people have jumped to the conclusion that you must feel angry when facing unfair situations. This writer believes that anger has the capacity to cloud people's ability to reason and behave effectively. You are not likely to think clearly when you are angry.

Try to remember the last time you felt extremely angry. Recall what you focused on and how you acted and then answer these questions:

- Were you able to calmly consider the best course of action?
- Were you able to look at all your options?
- Did you make the best decision?
- Do you regret something you said or did?

Holding on to anger is like grasping a hot coal with the intent of throwing it at someone else; you are the one who gets burned.

~Buddha

Gaining Control of Ourselves

Things work well when you are not angry

If you are like most people, you are probably intelligent and have good skills for resolving conflict and difficulties – when you are not angry. After you have cooled down, you can calmly identify and agree that you did not function at your best while in a state of rage.

Anger is not a universal tool

While anger may help in some situations, it is rarely helpful in making positive change or solving conflicts. Although anger is a normal human emotion, it is hardly the most useful for solving problems. Think about it and decide for yourself whether rage is helpful or harmful for you.

Anger Often Leads To Aggression

Another reason to control anger is that it can easily lead to aggression. Have you witnessed violence in your own life? Have you seen violence in the local news? Do you believe that our society is one of the most violent in the world? Do you know anyone who has been involved in physical violence?

According to recent statistics of the Federal Bureau of Investigation, one violent crime occurs in the United States every seventeen seconds. Acts of violence are particularly prevalent among teenagers. Murder or homicide is currently the second leading cause of death among ages 15-24, *making interpersonal violence one of the most important public health problems.*

Gaining Control of Ourselves

All forms of violence, including *road rage, desk rage, spousal abuse, child abuse, animal abuse, elder abuse and violence between children,* have reached epidemic proportions in the United States. Approximately 40% of women who are murdered in this country every year die at the hands of their boyfriends or husbands. Violence in families also takes a grim toll on young children. A government report concluded that, in the United States, approximately 140,000 children a year suffer serious injury from child abuse.

While anger does not automatically lead to aggression, it often does. It is frequently a blueprint for violence. For many of you, who may not have considered addressing this issue on your own, this course may well be an opportunity to improve your ability to manage intense emotions.

THE DROPS OF RAIN MAKE A HOLE IN THE STONE NOT BY VIOLENCE, BUT BY OFT FALLING.

-- LUCRETIUS

Personal/Self-Awareness Inventory

This assignment is designed to give you an opportunity to review your own typical ways of making choices about a range of issues. You may be surprised to discover the origin of your choices.

Section 1

1. What things do you do well?

2. Tell about a turning point in your life.

3. What has been the lowest point in your life?

4. Was there an event in which you demonstrated great courage?

5. Was there a time of heavy grief? More than one?

6. What do you do poorly but continue to do anyway?

7. What are some things you would like to stop doing?

8. What are some things you would really like to improve on?

9. Tell about some peak experience you have had. Tell about some peak experience you would like to have.

10. Are there some values you are struggling to establish?

11. Tell about one missed opportunity in your life.

Gaining Control of Ourselves

12. What are some things you want to start doing right at this point in your life?

13. What was the happiest period of your life?

Section 2

1. Do you like to take long walks alone? Where do you like to take your walks?

2. About how much money do you plan to spend on holiday gifts this year? Is this more or less than last year?

3. Do you watch TV? How much time do you spend watching TV in a week?

4. Which is more important to you, freedom or security?

5. What is your opinion on the "three-strikes-you're-out" law?

6. Do you have strong religious beliefs?

7. Is there anything special about family meals at your house?

8. What is your stand on birth-control devices or abortion?

9. How much do you like to give to charities, the poor, causes, *etc.*?

10. What do you plan on doing for your next vacation?

11. What did you do last night?

Gaining Control of Ourselves

12. Have you ever made a choice that surprised everyone?

13. If your parents are alive, how are you going to get involved in their lives when they get old?

14. What is one thing you would like to learn before you die?

15. How do you deal with unpleasant aspects of your work?

16. What brand of toothpaste do you use? How did you come to use this brand?

17. Did you ever write a letter to an editor of a newspaper or to a politician? What was the topic?

18. How important is an engagement ring if you plan to marry?

19. What are you saving money for?

20. Do you buy many music CDs? What kind?

21. Are you more or less religious now than you were three years ago?

22. Out of all the things you do in your free time, which one do you enjoy the most?

23. What activity do you least enjoy during your free time?

Gaining Control of Ourselves

Section 3

1. What does your family usually do for the holidays?

2. What have you done during the last two Thanksgiving vacations?

3. What have you done during the last two December vacations?

4. What magazines do you read regularly?

5. Do you subscribe to any magazines?

6. What are your favorite TV shows?

7. Do you keep up with the news or current events? What is your main source?

8. Have you seen any movies in the last few months? Tell us in a sentence or two about a movie you enjoyed and why you liked it?

9. What are your favorite sports?

10. What books have you read recently that you liked?

11. If you were a teacher, how would you teach your classes?

12. Do you have a hobby that you enjoy? What is it?

13. How did you first get involved in that hobby?

14. Do your friends enjoy similar hobbies?

Gaining Control of Ourselves

15. Are some of your friends not interested in your hobby?

16. What do your friends like about you?

17. Is there something you want badly but cannot afford right now? What is it?

18. Of all the people who have lent you a helping hand, who do you think made the biggest impact? How has this person helped you?

19. What are some things you really believe in?

20. What is the least enjoyable job you have had?

21. Where do you see yourself five years from now?

22. Are there injustices in your community you feel need to be changed?

23. Is there anything you would like to change about yourself? What would that be?

Section 4

1. Do you wear seat belts?

2. What are some of your notions of the good life?

Gaining Control of Ourselves

3. Do you smoke?

4. Are there things you would not tell even to one of your best friends? What kind of things?

5. Would you bring up your children differently from the way you were brought up? What would you do differently?

6. Did you ever steal anything? When? Why?

7. Do you ever get teased? Do you ever tease others?

8. What makes you dislike a person on sight?

9. Can you think of something that you would like to share with the group?

10. Do you feel satisfied with your life?

11. What improvements would you like to make in your life?

12. What is your main interest in life?

13. Describe something you have done recently to a person you dislike.

14. What do you do when you want to get out of a situation?

15. If you were given $5,000 what would you do with it?

16. In your estimation, are funerals important? Why?

17. How many children would you like to have?

18. How do you feel about interracial marriage?

19. How do you feel about homosexuality?

20. What celebrity would you like to have as a friend?

21. What disturbed you most about your parents when you were growing up?

22. What is your favorite color?

23. Are you satisfied with your height?

24. As a child, did you ever run away from home? Did you ever want to?

Section 5

1. Do you think you were an obedient child?

2. What was the most frightening thing that ever happened to you?

3. Do you believe in life after death?

Gaining Control of Ourselves

4. How often do you get in trouble?

5. How do you handle it when you get in trouble?

6. How do you think teachers should dress in school?

7. What is the worst thing you've ever done?

8. What is your favorite food?

9. How often do you eat out?

10. Do you cook? How often? What do you prepare?

11. Who makes your family's household decisions?

12. Please tell us about your family members.

13. What present would you like to receive?

14. Do you do things spontaneously or do you think things through before taking action?

15. Do you ever do things just because others expect you to do them?

16. Should people always do what they like to do?

17. How do you know when something is right or wrong?

18. Do you think a person should say something personal and/or embarrassing to another, e.g., that they have ripped pants?

19. If someone embarrassed you, what would you do?

20. Do you think the problems of pollution and traffic are being exaggerated?

21. If you could change one thing during your lifetime, what would that be?

22. Have you encountered a near-death experience?

Section 6

1. Do you have faith in our political system?

2. Are you proud of your work habits?

3. Are you proud of your accomplishments?

4. Do you actively practice your religious beliefs?

5. What are some of the things you are good at?

6. Have you ever written to a company complaining about a product?

7. What is the most stupid gift you have ever received for Christmas?

8. Have you ever tried to return a product to a store because it was defective?

Gaining Control of Ourselves

9. Do you feel your parents were fair?

10. Have you ever signed a petition? What was it?

11. Have you ever ridden on a motorcycle? Would you wear a helmet even if it was not required by law?

12. What would you do if you got too much change at the check-out counter?

13. Have you ever carried a picket sign?

14. What makes your best friend your best friend?

15. Do you know how to keep a checking account?

16. What is the one thing you want to do better?

17. Did you ever cheat at board games?

18. Do you like to get letters? Do you get letters?

19. Which was your best year in school?

20. Do you think you will ever dye your hair? Are you prejudiced against people who do?

21. If you were driving and came to a traffic signal where the light was red but no one was around, would you stop?

22. In what ways are you a conformist?

23. Have you ever read a book that had a deep effect on your life?

24. Do you think you are very materialistic?

The *free* expression of the hopes and aspirations of a people is the greatest and only safety in a sane society.

– Emma Goldman

Peace is not merely a distant goal that we seek, but a means by which we arrive at that goal.

– Martin Luther King, jr.

Gaining Control of Ourselves

NOTES:

Gaining Control of Ourselves

Part 2: Stress Management

It is important to remember that small hassles of everyday life can cause a lot of stress. When we speak of stress, what we are usually describing is a set of symptoms that may vary from one person to another. *Upset stomach, nervous feelings, constant fatigue, tight neck muscles, depression* and *headaches* are some of the most common symptoms.

Some stress in normal

Stress is a normal part of everyday life. Everyone experiences anxiety, tension and pressures at school, work, or home. A certain amount of stress in life is good. It keeps us energized, motivated, and productive. However, too much stress or stress experienced over a prolonged period of time without relief can be harmful to both your physical and mental health. Stress is our body's natural response to danger or what we think is a threat. When we sense danger, our heart rate increases, our blood pressure rises and we are prepared for *"fight, flight, or freeze."* In a later chapter, we will see that the exact same reactions occur when we experience anger.

Is it worth dying for?

No matter what symptoms you experience, excessive stress can be hazardous to your health. Research has found that stress is linked to potentially fatal conditions such as heart attacks, cancer, and a decline in the immune system, which makes your body more susceptible to infection and disease.

One Step at a time

Learning to manage stress is a four step process. The steps involve:

1. Developing awareness that you are becoming stressed.
2. Identifying situations that result in feeling stressed.
3. Learning effective coping techniques.
4. Practicing the first three steps.

Gaining Control of Ourselves

You have a choice

In addition to learning to recognize the signs and symptoms of stress, you can also develop an understanding and ability to utilize skills to either *accept, cope with,* or *change* your stressors. It is necessary to be realistic about the source of your stress; if it is caused by something beyond your control, your alternative may be limited to *acceptance*. When stress is caused by something you can control, however, you can take action to change the situation. The ability to accept, cope with, and change, leads to effective stress management, whereas, the inability to adapt may result in physiological or mental disorders.

What Is Stress?

Stress is a *mismatch* between the *demands* in our lives and the *resources* we have to deal with those demands. The stressor could be a positive or a negative occurrence. The type of response produced depends on the individual's reaction to the stressor.

Stress is Physical

When we are under stress, our bodies react with the *"fight, flight, or freeze"* response. Adrenaline and other chemicals are pumped into the bloodstream. Breathing becomes shallow and rapid, muscles tense up and your body prepares for action. In most cases, though, the body is all geared up with no place to go. If we do nothing to reverse the physical stress reaction, we can remain in an almost constant state of *unproductive tension*.

Stress is Mental

Stress is not all in your head, but that is where it begins. Different individuals perceive stressors differently. For one person, an event may be viewed as a challenge; for another, it may be viewed as a severe threat or problem. **Therefore, events do not cause stress,** *the ways we interpret and react to them does.*

Gaining Control of Ourselves

Stress May Be Beneficial

Many people do their best work under pressure. A moderate degree of stress is a powerful force for growth; we often learn the most when we are forced to do so. Some students do their best studying when they have a deadline to meet. Athletes report that they sometimes have an adrenaline "rush" when they need it most.

Stress May Be Harmful

Stress hurts when it becomes a way of life. The accumulated effects of long-term stress have been linked to heart disease, ulcers, cancer, anxiety disorders, and depression. Under stressful situations, the entire muscle structure tends to constrict. Sometimes, when the heart and arteries constrict, this can result in strokes or heart attacks.

Three Skills for Managing Stress

The three skills for managing stress are:

1. **Awareness** of what causes stress in your life.

2. **Acceptance** of what you can do about it.

3. **Coping** with the stressors.

> Have patience with all things, but chiefly have patience with yourself. Do not lose courage in considering your own imperfections, but instantly set about remedying them – every day begin the task anew.
>
> – St. Francis de Sales

Gaining Control of Ourselves

Skill 1: Awareness
Identifying Your Stressors

What causes stress in your life? We usually think of stressors as events that make us angry or upset. They may be situations that make us sad, frightened, unsure, startled, excited or happy. We may even cause our own stress through our thoughts, feelings and expectations. Any event or thought that brings about strong emotions, negative or positive, has the potential to cause stress. It may also come from the combination of small hassles in our lives.

Check the list

Some common stress-causing events are listed below. It may be helpful for you to review the following list of commonly identified factors to determine if any of these may pose a threat to your continued growth or functioning. Once you identify your possible high-risk factors, you can then begin to plan prevention strategies to help you handle these without aggression. Put a check mark beside the factor that you can relate to, and add any others you can think of at the bottom.

WHICH OF THE FOLLOWING FACTORS COULD BE A CAUSE OF STRESS FOR YOU?

- ❑ Unable to express angry feelings (*i.e.* holding anger in, expressing it inappropriately or aggressively)
- ❑ Exhaustion or fatigue
- ❑ Family
- ❑ School
- ❑ Difficulty with time management
- ❑ Losing
- ❑ Being cut off in traffic
- ❑ Too much responsibility and too little control over events
- ❑ Anger about things over which you have no control
- ❑ Loneliness or isolating yourself from others
- ❑ Never getting a fair share
- ❑ Overwhelmed because so many exciting things are happening to you
- ❑ Short of money
- ❑ Feeling helpless or hopeless
- ❑ Too many assignments to complete at once
- ❑ Pressures to do things you feel you're unable to do
- ❑ Others: _____

_____
_____

Gaining Control of Ourselves

Recognizing your stress symptoms

What is your body trying to tell you about stress? Many of us do not recognize warning signs when they occur. Physical symptoms, emotions, or certain kinds of behavior can be signs of stress; a few are listed below. Think about which symptoms you experience, and add others that are not on the list.

PHYSICAL	EMOTIONAL	BEHAVIORAL
Tight muscles	Depression	Overeating
Pounding heart	Anger	More drinking
Chest pain	Irritability	Road rage
Headaches	Low self-esteem	Inattention
High blood pressure	Apathy	Forgetfulness
Upset stomach	Negativity	Smoking
Fatigue	Impatience	Less sex
Others:		

Gaining Control of Ourselves

Know the signs

The combinations of stress symptoms frequently drive people into action. If you recognize these traits in yourself, be aware that they can make you more prone to disease because your immune system breaks down. ***The first step in managing stress is to recognize it.*** Once you have thought about the cause and symptoms, you are ready to connect the two. Each event that sets off a stress response in you is a stressor. In this section we teach and encourage participants to talk about angry or upsetting feelings rather than to act upon them.

WHAT HAPPENED?	HOW I REACTED (Feelings/Behavior)
My supervisor/teacher criticized my work.	Angry/My stomach was upset all afternoon.
A driver cut me off in traffic.	Outraged/I yelled out the window and flipped him the finger.
A worker from a previous shift left work for me which should have been completed during their shift.	I became upset and started an argument with my supervisor.
My brother/sister left a chore for me which they should have done.	I got really angry and threatened my sister/brother.

Learn To Recognize and Control Your Thoughts
Stress is not always a reaction to a specific situation. Often, our thoughts can lead to intense feelings of stress. Have you ever noticed how uptight you feel when you are caught up in your thinking? When your mind is racing, one thought leads to another, and yet another, until at some point, you become incredibly agitated. The solution is to notice what's happening in your head before your thoughts have a chance to build any momentum. The sooner you catch yourself in the act of building your mental snowball or mind tornado, the easier it is to stop.

If you can imagine another world, you are already beginning to build towards it.

- Luis J. Rodriguez

Gaining Control of Ourselves

Please try the following exercise:

- Think of everything you have to do tomorrow. Summarize your thoughts in the space below.

- List each thought that came to your mind.

- Pay attention to the way you feel as your thoughts keep building. Write your responses (feelings, body symptoms) you experienced in relation to each thought.

    1. Thought:

    ➢ *Feelings/Body Symptoms:*

    2. Thought:

    ➢ *Feelings/Body Symptoms:*

    3. Thought:

    ☞ *Feelings/Body Symptoms:*

Gaining Control of Ourselves

Describe how it feels to build your mental snowball. Does it make you feel calm? Or does it make you feel even more stressed than you were when you started?

Review your responses. Circle any of the feelings or body symptoms that you would like to avoid or eliminate. For each one, write a few lines about the changes you would like to make.

Is the glass half empty or half full? It's your choice

List some of the ways in which you might stop this train of thought before it has a chance to get going. For example, rather than focusing on how overwhelmed you are, think of how grateful you are for remembering what needs to be done to correct the situation.

A pessimist is one who makes difficulties of his opportunities and an optimist is one who makes opportunities of his difficulties.

– Harry Truman

Skill 2: Acceptance

> Worrying about the future is about as effective as trying to solve an algebra equation by chewing bubble gum.
>
> – Mary Schmich

Have you ever worried about the weather? How much good did it do? Sometimes the only thing we can do is to learn to take things as they are. When a situation cannot be controlled or influenced, we must use self-talk to position ourselves to appropriately accept the situation with the least amount of damage to ourselves.

Keep Situations in Perspective

Of all the things you worried about during the past year, how many came true? Most of your fears probably never came true. Many of us worry about things that never happen. We put unnecessary stress on ourselves by over dramatizing ("This is going to blow my future.") or exaggerating the reaction of others ("They will all hate me if I do that!"). When worries and fears are causing you a lot of stress, use self-talk and ask yourself:

- Has this happened before?
- What did I learn from that experience?
- What is the worst possible outcome? (*Be realistic!*)
- What else can I do?
- What advice would I give to a friend in this situation?
- Five years from now will I even remember this event?
- Is this event likely to change the course of history?

Gaining Control of Ourselves

Use Self-Dialogue

Many people find that repeating certain phrases to themselves helps them accept things or calm down. Below are some examples. Choose (or invent) one as a "secret strategy" to use against bad or upsetting times.

- Someday we will laugh about this.
- It is a learning experience.
- Things could be worse.
- I will get over it.
- Calm down.
- Every cloud has a silver lining.
- Take things day by day.
- This does not mean it's the end of the world.
- I have handled more serious situations in the past.
- I can make a plan to handle this.
- What is it I have to do?
- It will be over shortly.
- It is natural for my fear to rise.
- It's getting better each time I use self-talk.
- *Invent one:* _____

_____

It is a good idea to refresh your self-statement list periodically, removing and adding new self-statements. You can list them on the back of a business card to keep with you. It is important to remember that practice makes perfect.

Keep a Positive Attitude

It is hard to smile when things are going wrong. There are times when you need to blow off steam or express your resentment. But letting negative emotions take over completely only makes the situation worse. If you focus on the positives, you're more likely to find a way out. A positive attitude can become contagious, making it easier to live and work with others. In times of stress, it is better to spend time with

Gaining Control of Ourselves

people who are positive rather than those who tend to see the worst of every issue.

Develop a "Stress-Resistant" Personality

Below is a list of traits common among people who have not developed a stress-resistant personality. These traits may trigger a stress reaction:

- Unrealistic expectations.
- Constant dissatisfaction.
- Inability to relax.
- Always in a hurry.
- Constantly worrying about little things.
- Making things seem worse than they really are.

How to develop a stress-resistant personality:

- Getting regular (non-competitive) exercise.
- Consider problems as challenges.
- Look for possibilities and creative solutions.
- Buffer stress with a commitment to family, friends, religious and community activities.
- Develop a support group by getting involved and keeping in touch with others.
- Getting proper rest.
- Learn to be helpful and give to others.

Try to accept the fact that the reality of life is that things don't always work the way we want or expect. People who are always rushing and pushing often accomplish less than people who take time to plan and relax.

I think the next best thing to solving a problem is finding some humor int it.
  – Frank A. Clark

Gaining Control of Ourselves

Get Counseling

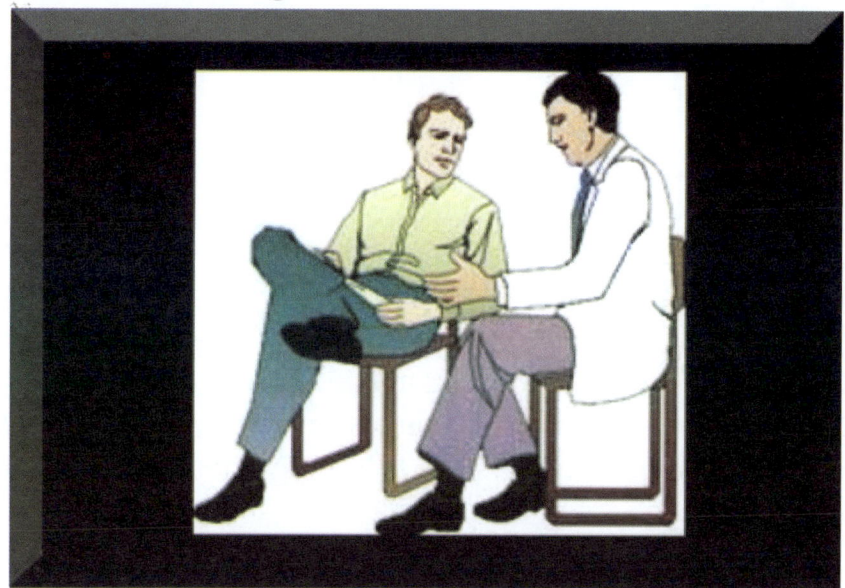

Stress is the basis of all mental disorders and is the source of many physical illnesses. Sometimes the only way to deal with the effects of a stressful event is to get professional help. Seeking counseling or psychotherapy is not a sign of weakness; it takes strength to recognize that you cannot always do it alone. Learn to make use of, not avoid, external help. Many companies have free counseling through their Employee Assistance Program. Depression is often the result of unmanaged stress, yet it is successfully treated in 80% of all cases. Counseling for emotional problems should not be seen as a stigma but rather a wise choice for a thoughtful person.

Skill 3: Coping Skills

There are many ways to move away from or reduce the effects of stress. You can literally "run away" from stress: swim, bike or walk. Physical fitness helps fight stress in two ways:

- A physically fit body is better able to withstand the effects of stress. A well-balanced fitness program that includes good nutrition and adequate sleep gives you energy and endurance to handle whatever comes your way. You may want to consider a change in your life style to help reduce your level of stress.

- Exercise has a calming effect that lasts long after the exercise session is over. Repetitive exercise like running and swimming can produce a mental state similar to that produced by meditation. Aerobic exercise that gets your heart pounding for at least 20 minutes releases chemicals in the brain (called endorphins) that reduce depression and stress. Non-aerobic stretching exercises like yoga are also calming because they induce deep breathing and a meditation-like mental state.

Gaining Control of Ourselves

Just Do It!
- Take a walk, play at the beach, work in the yard, and shoot some hoops.
- Go for a jog.
- Swim a few laps.
- Roll your shoulders, raise them to your ears.
- Play music which helps you relax.

Relaxation
Many of the ways we "relax"–drinking, smoking, watching TV, eating–do nothing to reverse the physical effects of stress. In fact, smoking actually produces a stress response by narrowing blood vessels and releasing chemicals into the bloodstream. Drinking actually causes a depressed mood, which is the last thing one needs at times of stress.

You can learn to relax
True relaxation is a skill that you can learn and use when you need it. Stress causes the following body reactions:

- tenses your body
- makes your breathing shallow
- raises your blood pressure
- makes your heart pound
- clouds your judgment

Learning relaxation skills, and using the techniques, can reverse the physical and emotional effects of stress by helping you physically feel better, think more clearly, and improve your mood.

☞ You can out-distance that which is running after you, but not what is running inside you.

– Rwandan Proverb

☞ A child becomes an adult when he realizes that he has a right not only to be right, but also to be wrong.

– Thomas Szusz

Gaining Control of Ourselves

Get away from it all

If you imagine yourself to be "stressed out," you surely will be. When you are feeling stressed, go to a quiet place and try the following steps to reduce your stress level:

1. Sit or lie in a comfortable position.
2. Breathe deeply and slowly, in through your nose, out through your mouth.
3. Mentally scan your body for the most relaxed areas.
4. Start with your feet and work up through your legs, buttocks, torso, shoulders, arms, neck and head.
5. Let your jaw drop.
6. Allow your eyelids to be heavy and relaxed.
7. At places where you feel relaxation, take a deep, full breath and imagine the relaxation expanding when you exhale.
8. Continue to breathe slowly and regularly. Think "*peace*" during the inhale and "*release*" during the exhale.
9. Once you feel relaxed, enjoy it.
10. Imagine you are in a beautiful place – a beach, a forest, a mountaintop or any place that pleases you.
11. Remain in this relaxed state for 5 to 10 minutes.
12. Allow your thoughts to pass through your mind without paying much attention to them.
13. Use "self-talk" to relax even further.
14. Repeat the following to yourself:

    *"I am relaxed and calm,
    my hands are heavy and warm,
    my heartbeat is slow and regular
    I feel peaceful and still."*

This may sound like a lot of things to remember, but with a little practice it can become part of your normal stress relief routine.

Gaining Control of Ourselves

Reflect On What We Have Learned

1. Which stress management technique(s) do you see yourself using?

2. What is the most valuable lesson you have learned so far?

3. How do you manage your stress?

4. Have you seen any changes in yourself?

5. Which is the most helpful stress management technique for you?

6. Why do you think it works?

> *Giving up doesn't always mean you are weak. Sometimes it means that you are strong enough to let go.*

Gaining Control of Ourselves

NOTES:

Another Way of Managing Stress:

Systematic Desensitization

The **first** thing you must realize is how your body reacts to stressful situations. Muscles tense, blood pressure is elevated, and breathing becomes faster. The emotional feeling that often occurs along with the physiological changes is *irritability*. At this point, "blowing up" or "venting" because of frustrations is common—this is negative and counterproductive. It is important to be aware of your reactions to stressful situations and to replace "dysfunctional" responses with healthier, more adjusted activities. "Relaxation responses" are techniques that teach people how to relax and reduce tension during stressful situations. These techniques, such as muscle relaxation, meditation, and "time-out," are learned, practiced, and used as mounting tensions are recognized. Practice the "Getting away from it All" technique on page 41.

Frustration meter

The **second** step is to identify events you know are stressful or anxiety provoking to you. List ten situations where you have "blown up," "vented," or felt "out of control." Place these ten in order from *least* frustrating to *most* frustrating. This is called a hierarchy of stressful events.

1. _____
2. _____
3. _____
4. _____
5. _____
6. _____
7. _____
8. _____
9. _____
10. _____

Gaining Control of Ourselves

The **third** step is to practice these techniques in a safe environment. After identifying these stressful events or situations, and after practicing relaxation responses, apply the technique. Begin by either imagining or role-playing yourself in the least frustrating situation and gradually progressing to more stressful situations. Only progress to the next situation when you feel comfortable with the level of adjustment to the current stressful event on which you are working.

Step **four** requires that you practice the technique in real-life situations. Just as in the third step, you must gradually work your way up the stressful events hierarchy, from the least stressful situation to the most. When first using the systematic desensitization technique in a real-life situation, it is advisable to practice in situations where you are not "trapped" and from which you can walk away at any time, or take a time-out.

How Well Do You Manage Stress?

How good are your stress-management skills? The following questions will help you pinpoint areas where you are doing fine, and identify areas where you need improvement.

1. List three situations that cause stress in your life.
    -
    -
    -

2. List three symptoms (physical, emotional or behavioral) that occur when you are under stress.
    -
    -
    -

Gaining Control of Ourselves

Acceptance Skill Questions

Please write a brief comment under each question explaining your response.

1. Are you able to maintain a positive or neutral attitude and keep from getting upset over "little" things?

2. Can you sometimes talk yourself out of feeling stressed?

3. To what extent can you anticipate stressful situations and apply prevention strategies to protect yourself?

Coping Skill Questions

1. Do you know (and use) relaxation techniques like deep breathing or meditation?

2. When you feel stressed, do you ever exercise to get rid of this feeling?

Action Skill Questions

1. Do you make a list and prioritize tasks to keep yourself from feeling too rushed?

2. How do you plan your activities to avoid or reduce stress?

Communication Skill Questions

1. Are you able to express your feelings easily?

2. Can you communicate effectively with others when conflicts arise?

3. Are you able to listen to others with a sense of concern and caring?

Gaining Control of Ourselves

Become A Better Listener

Are you content to listen to the *entire* thought of someone else rather than waiting impatiently for your chance to respond? If so, then you are an effective listener.

Check your listening skill below. This true/false exercise will help you isolate your problem areas.

	A	B
I'm not good at following verbal travel directions.	[ ] F	[ ] T
Before responding to what someone has told me, I restate in my own words what they said.	[ ] T	[ ] F
I forget people's names almost as soon as I learn them.	[ ] F	[ ] T
Most people equate slow responses to questions with slow thinking.	[ ] F	[ ] T
I tend to doodle or fidget when on the telephone.	[ ] F	[ ] T
In conversations I find myself mostly answering questions.	[ ] F	[ ] T
People find me easy to talk to.	[ ] T	[ ] F
People often ask me for advice.	[ ] T	[ ] F
I usually ask a lot of questions when I am in a conversation.	[ ] T	[ ] F
While someone is talking to me, I am mentally preparing my response before they are finished.	[ ] T	[ ] T

Total column A: _____   Total column B: _____   Score is A – B: _____

Interpretation:

Score greater than +1: You have already developed a number of listening skills and with practice can master effective listening.

Score +1 through -1: Your listening ability is about average. Training in communication skills can help you master effective listening.

Score below -1: Your ability to listen effectively can use some improvement. Pay close attention to mastering communication skills.

Gaining Control of Ourselves

Think about the best listener you know. List the qualities that make him or her a good listener:

Circle the qualities you share with this person. Concentrate on improving upon the qualities you did not circle.

_____

Think about the worst listener you know. List the behaviors that make it clear this person is not hearing what you are saying:

Circle the qualities you share with this person. Work on eliminating these habits from your own listening.

_____

List how better listening skills will help you in these situations.

- At work/school:

- In your relationships:

- In social situations:

Gaining Control of Ourselves

Stress Log

Please use the Stress Log to keep track of the stressors and responses you notice throughout the day. This journal will be used as a measurement of how you have changed and in what areas you still have room for growth.

What Happened...(Situation)	How I Reacted...(Changes)

Gaining Control of Ourselves

For each stressor in your stress log, ask yourself two questions:

- How important is it?
- Can you control the event?

Put each stressor in the appropriate box below.

Important / Controllable   **Example:** *You are chronically late.*
Important / Uncontrollable   **Example:** *Someone you love has terminal cancer.*
Unimportant / Controllable   **Example:** *You think you have a bad hair day.*
Unimportant / Uncontrollable   **Example:** *You think that you are too short.*

IMPORTANT / CONTROLLABLE	UNIMPORTANT / CONTROLLABLE
IMPORTANT / UNCONTROLLABLE	**UNIMPORTANT / UNCONTROLLABLE**

☞ For fast acting relief, try to slow down.
    – Lily Tomlin

☞ Vitality shows in not only the ability to persist, but the ability to start over.
    – F. Scott Fitzgerald

Gaining Control of Ourselves

Strategies to Handle High-Risk Situations

Choose two high-risk situations you are concerned about now. Identify your physical, emotional, and behavioral reactions to the stressor. Write the situations below and identify three coping strategies or ways you can handle these without resorting to aggression.

HIGH-RISK SITUATION 1 – *Related Facts and Information*

Coping Strategy 1:

Coping Strategy 2:

Coping Strategy 3:

HIGH-RISK SITUATION 2 – *Related Facts and Information*

Coping Strategy 1:

Coping Strategy 2:

Coping Strategy 3:

Review: Stress Test

1. What is stress?

2. List three skills you can use to manage stress:

3. Name two physical symptoms of stress:

4. Name two emotional or behavioral symptoms of stress:

We have already discussed that "stress is physical." By that we mean that when we are under stress, our bodies react with the "fight, flight, or freeze" response. Adrenaline and other chemicals are pumped into the bloodstream. Breathing becomes shallow, muscles tense up, and the body prepares for action.

5. What is meant by the statement "stress is beneficial?" Give an example.

6. What is meant by the statement "stress is harmful?" Give an example.

7. What does the statement "stress is energy" mean? Give an example.

8. What causes stress in your life?

Gaining Control of Ourselves

NOTES:

Part 3: Emotional Intelligence

Emotional intelligence is a new concept, which is related to **the ability to understand one's own feelings and behavior as well as the capacity to sense the feelings and needs of others and to utilize this information in a way that enhances interpersonal relationships**. Emotional Intelligence is also the capacity to create positive outcomes in your relationships with others and yourself. Positive outcomes include joy, optimism, and success in work, school, and life. Increasing emotional intelligence has been correlated with better results in leadership, sales, software development, academic performance, marriage, friendships, and overall health.

In this class, it is our goal to assist you in developing an understanding of your strengths and weaknesses and assist in improving your capability in this area. We encourage you to use your instincts, hunches and feelings along with available facts and information to guide your decisions. Recognizing and understanding your feelings and emotions and managing their impact on other people must be practiced between classes to internalize the skills being taught. We believe that it is important to take an interest in people and learn to listen to their views, problems and concerns. Listening is important in communication and is a skill that can be taught.

Emotions: Our guidance system

Nature developed our emotions over millions of years of evolution. As a result, our emotions have the potential to serve us today as a guidance system. Our emotions let us know when any natural human need is not being met. For example, when we feel lonely, our need for connection with other people is unmet. When we feel afraid, our need for safety is unmet. When we feel rejected, it is our need for acceptance that is unmet.

Gaining Control of Ourselves

Perception is everything

The way we *appraise* (see) our environment at any given time is important in determining how we respond emotionally. If we appraise a situation as a threat, put-down, or an insult, we are more likely to respond with anger. If we appraise a situation positively, our response will be positive. Two people can appraise the same situation differently. Our feelings are very personal and do not follow rules of logic. We can appraise the same situation differently at different times based on our moods, level of stress, and clarity of thought, and consequently respond differently.

Emotions are important

Our emotions are a useful source of information. Our emotions help us make decisions. Studies show that when a person has an accident in which the portion of the brain that deals with emotions is damaged he cannot make even simple decisions. Why? Because he doesn't know how he will feel about his choices.

Our bodies talk

Our emotions help us communicate with others. Our facial expressions, for example, can convey a wide range of emotions. If we look sad or hurt, we are letting the other person know that we need their help. If we are verbally skilled we will be able to express more of our emotional needs and thereby have a better chance of filling them. If we are good at listening to the emotional needs of others, we are better able to help them feel understood, important, and cared about. The emotionally intelligent person is able to read, with some accuracy, the feelings conveyed non-verbally by those with whom he or she interacts.

Stress reduces our ability to feel

As our society has become more pressured and we are constantly overwhelmed by stress, our ability to recognize and respond to our own feelings and those of others is diminished. Overwhelming feelings of stress result in a reduced ability to manage intense feelings and an increase in stress-related disorders. Consequently, there is an increase in road rage, desk rage, aggression, violence against others, substance abuse, and other inappropriate displays of anger.

Gaining Control of Ourselves

Emotions bring people together

Our emotions are perhaps the greatest potential source of uniting all members of the human race. This is what makes us human. Clearly, our various religious, cultural and political beliefs have not united us. Far too often, in fact, they have even divided us. Emotions, on the other hand, are universal.
The emotions of

- **Empathy**
  The ability to understand someone else's feelings.

- **Compassion**
  The ability to care about and give to someone else.

- **Cooperation**
  The ability to work together to achieve a common goal.

- **Forgiveness**
  The ability to pardon someone for a grievance against you or against someone one or something you care about.

All of these emotions have the potential to unite us as people. Our thoughts may tend to divide us, whereas our emotions, if given the chance, will unite us.

Develop an Understanding of Yourself

Emotions are an important aspect of every person. We believe that there are around eight basic feelings, which everyone experiences from time to time. These feelings are:

1. anger
2. sorrow
3. fear
4. love
5. joy
6. acceptance
7. disgust
8. surprise

Instead of disconnecting our emotions, we need to control our actions.

Gaining Control of Ourselves

Feelings have names

We experience these feelings in many variations each day. These emotions may blend or conflict. If we learn to understand our feelings, name them, and begin to understand their causes and effects, they help us gain a greater ability to manage our behavior in any given situation. Our brains and bodies influence our behavior.

Recognize Patterns of Behavior

Our brain follows patterns, or pathways. First there is an action (stimulus), which leads to a response, and over time, the response becomes almost automatic. Once this occurs, it requires conscious effort to change or interrupt the automatic process.

Push my buttons

You could think of your brain as a juke box where most of your records (your reactions to different situations) are recorded before you enter adolescence. Then as life goes on and someone pushes your buttons, you play the record that fits the situation. It's an automatic response!

Our beliefs control our behavior

These brain patterns lead to behavior patterns. At a young age, we learn lessons from our families of how to cope, how to get our needs met, and how to protect ourselves. These strategies reinforce one another, and we develop a complex structure of beliefs to support the reasonableness of our behaviors.

> *There's no operation where you can have your anger cut out. But if you work on yourself, as you get better, you'll be more capable of seeing others as flawed human beings. That makes it easier to forgive.*
>
> – Robin Quivers

Gaining Control of Ourselves

You can change if you want to

As we become more conscious of the patterns we exhibit, it becomes possible to:

- Analyze these beliefs and replace them if they are inappropriate.

- Interrupt the pattern and replace it with conscious behavior that moves us closer to our real goals.

This is simple, but it's not easy. It is a task that requires hard work and a desire to change–but it is not difficult to begin. It can be as simple as taking a brief pause to allow the conscious brain to begin to intervene in the pattern.

Learn to Think of Consequences

Teachers, parents, and others often tell us to control our emotions and cut them off from the decision-making process, especially feelings of anger and fear. For example "don't let your anger guide your action." This sounds easy but it is neither practical nor realistic.

Use your mind and your heart

Feelings provide us with a guide to action, energy, and the real basis for almost every decision. Instead of disconnecting our emotions, we need to control our actions so that we have time to make the most creative, insightful, and powerful decisions. This is especially true when dealing with conflict or crisis. We need to slow down the process and apply carefully practiced strategies that lead to decisions informed by the combination of our mind and our hearts. All of these concepts can be learned and are designed to lead to an increase in emotional intelligence.

The willingness to accept responsibility for one's own life is the source from which self-respect springs.
— Joan Didion

Cause and effect

This new habit pattern limits impulsive behavior by giving us a clear understanding of the consequences of our choices and the ability to imagine the cause and effect relationships. As we are more able to control our own actions, we become more capable of influencing the behavior of persons with whom we interact.

One important element needed to develop and monitor consequential thinking is "self-talk." Self-talk is a technique used to mentally explore multiple options and viewpoints; providing a system to balance the various aspects of our thoughts and feelings. Just as in conversations with others, the skill of "listening" to verbal and non-verbal communication is important. Listening to the messages sent from your own thoughts and feelings is also helpful in thinking through and anticipating consequences.

Self-talk works

This may seem like a difficult technique to understand and master, however, participants who practice it over time agree that it actually works. Examples of self-talk are covered in more detail in a later chapter of this publication.

Ask for and Listen to Advice

In our daily lives, we have countless opportunities to get feedback about our thoughts, feelings, and actions. This feedback can suggest a need for change. If we listen, it can be used to make adjustments in our behavior. Unfortunately, we don't always listen. Instead we often ignore useful feedback or information. Ignoring feedback from others results in a lack of self-awareness. When that happens we become prone to severing connections with our basic goodness, becoming selfish, and allowing ourselves to be controlled by automatic responses, bad habits, or addictions.

Gaining Control of Ourselves

Listen to those around you

It is important to learn how our inner dialogs with ourselves shape our feelings and actions. Participants must engage in an activity that helps them become aware of the self-talk associated with an issue that they find particularly troublesome or disturbing. The alternative is to listen to ourselves and to others who have our interests at heart. When we become skilled at sensing our own emotions and listening to them, we are able to tap into the energy they provide and take the best action. *Emotional intelligence can be increased with practice.*

You learned it on the playground

Emotions are energy, and one place where energy most frequently erupts is in conflict. Conflict is natural in interactions with others. You can easily see that by looking at a group of preschoolers on the playground to observe this in action. In order to manage conflict we develop skills for evaluation, negotiation, and compromise. To socialize effectively you must recognize and gauge other peoples' thoughts, feelings, tone, facial expression, and body language, just as you monitor your own feelings and actions. These skills are heavily dependent on interpreting the various forms of non-verbal communication. Through practice, the skill of becoming effective in turning conflict into a positive force is improved. The ability to create compromise and make sure needs are met is further developed. The skill of mobilizing, persuading, and inspiring others are acquired.

Role models are important

The most critical step in teaching and learning effective socialization is to provide positive role models and opportunities for children to practice what they have observed. Today, children often do not see their parents' interactions socially nor do they share as many opportunities to practice social skills with extended family including grandparents, cousins, aunts and uncles. Therefore, it is even more important that parents provide these role models and opportunities for practice.

Consistency counts

Children also need to be responsible and accountable for their decisions and actions. With young children, it is important to intervene immediately and provide alternative ways of handling differences. You need to continue your actions with words, and you need to be consistent.

Gaining Control of Ourselves

Motivation is Key to Change

"Motivation" comes from the Latin word for "to move." It is a goal-oriented behavior. In essence, we take action because it feels good to do so. It feels right to take a break when we are on overload, then it feels right to go back to work. The real challenge is to make it feel right to take action that does not have an immediate reward. For teenagers, and young adults, it is natural to want to see immediate results from any action. Their brains are still developing the ability to reason from cause to effect. In order to feel motivated, we have to tap into the part of ourselves that has a longer view, which also feels right.

Take the long view

All of us make countless decisions every hour. What should I eat for lunch? Which book should I read first? Should I do homework? Which person should I ask? In part, we make those decisions unconsciously based on our patterns and habits – the things we learned from our families. We also make decisions based on our personal priorities. So, if we want to redirect our decision to take a longer view, we need to both *shape unconscious habits* and *examine priorities* to make sure they match. Therefore, completing the assignments between sessions are far more likely to lead to permanent change than the time spent in the sessions.

Creating the correct environment can motivate others

In addition to motivating ourselves, it is important to learn how to create an environment where others can become motivated. There are many ways to do so. The most obvious is "extrinsic" motivation. For example, "If you carry my books, I will give you part of my lunch," is a simple example of extrinsic motivation. It is a bribe or an offer made in exchange for a service. Regardless of how it is viewed, both parties benefit in some way.

Increase Empathy

Empathy is the ability to recognize and respond to other peoples' emotions. It is connected to optimism because it is through a sense of our connection to others that we see our own sense of well-being and importance. Another word for this is "conscience." Together they govern a large part of our behavior. They are the gatekeepers of our emotional selves. When we are empathic, it affects us when we hurt others or to see them hurt. We actually experience for ourselves the emotions of others. It becomes a motivation not only to do what makes us feel good, but also what makes others feel good. Thus, empathy is the force that makes the Golden Rule true.

Gaining Control of Ourselves

It starts at birth

Some parts of empathy are instinctive. Infants will reach out and touch others in distress. In maternity wards, one infant's tears will lead to a room full of crying babies. This mimicry is the first step toward forming empathy.

Connection is important

Unfortunately, this unconscious or instinctive behavior does not automatically lead to conscious empathy. Instead, these seeds must be nurtured through role modeling, reinforcement, and practice. Once people develop empathy on a conscious level, it becomes natural and self-reinforcing because it fulfills a deep-seated need to connect with others.

Managing Negative Emotions

General Guidelines

Emotions that lead to negative consequences should be recognized and managed in order to avoid situations that may be hurtful to you or someone else. Here are some guidelines that may help you manage negative emotions:

1. Identify the feeling.
2. Ask if it is healthy.
3. If it's not healthy work to replace it or put it out of your mind.

<u>Ask yourself, of the things I can control, what would help me feel better?</u>
List your options and choose the one most likely to lead to your long-term happiness. While you cannot and should not attempt to control anyone else, you can and are obligated to control yourself. One of the keys in self-control is thinking before acting. While this seems simple, it is a skill that needs to be practiced and made a part of your usual daily functioning.

~~~~~~~~~

Grant me the serenity to accept the things I cannot change,
The courage to change the things I can,
And the Wisdom to know the difference.

Gaining Control of Ourselves

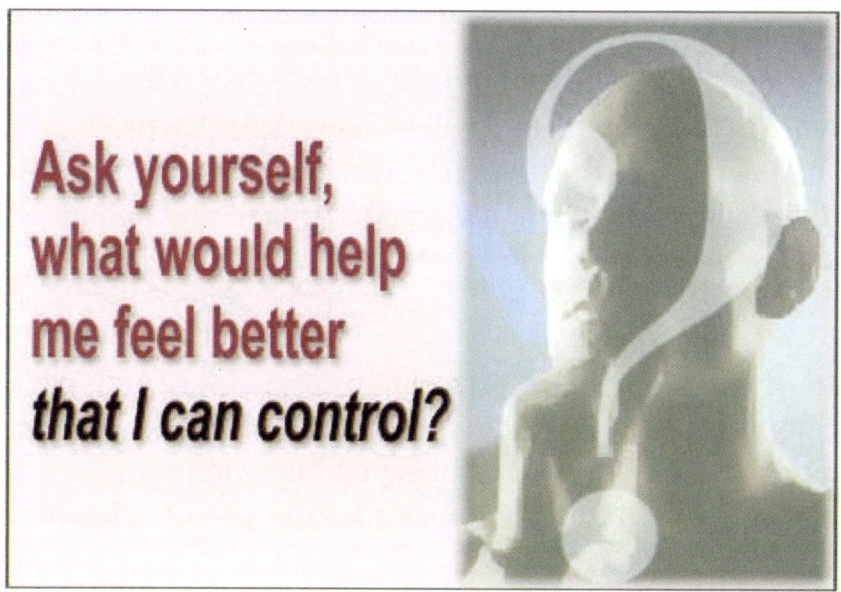

List the items that you can control in your life:

1. _____
2. _____
3. _____
4. _____
5. _____
6. _____
7. _____

Of the items listed above which ones will help you gain long term happiness?

_____
_____
_____
_____
_____
_____
_____

Depression

Like anger, depression is a *secondary emotion*. By this we mean that there are always other feelings which contribute to and cause depression. Depression is an important symptom to understand, as it is often depression, stress or fear, which is the source of anger. Since depression is not always recognized and understood, it often places the sufferer at a disadvantage in responding appropriately.

Negatives mount up

For example, a person might feel lonely, rejected, discouraged, grieved, unfulfilled, irritated, disconnected, uninspired, unproductive, unaccomplished, uncertain, misunderstood, or pessimistic. Together, all of these feelings drain their energy, kill their motivation, and cause them to feel depressed. Poor physical health can also cause depression.

Divided they fall

It is often helpful to isolate each feeling, and then take action by thinking about a plan to attack each negative feeling individually. In each case ask, "What would help me feel less lonely, unproductive, discouraged or depressed."

Gaining Control of Ourselves

Here are some questions that might help you assess your own depression:

1. Have I lost something?
   - A belief, a dream, a relationship, a vision?
   - Is there some unmet expectation?
   - Unfulfilled desire?

2. Am I feeling productive?
   - Am I accomplishing anything?

3. Do I feel focused?
   - Do I have any goals that I am working towards?

4. Am I feeling pessimistic about something?
   - About several things?
   - Am I discouraged about something?
   - Hopeless?

5. What beliefs are helping me feel pessimistic, discouraged, or hopeless?

6. Am I looking for something on the outside to happen before I will feel better?

7. Am I feeling dependent on someone?

8. Do I feel resentful about something?
   - About someone?

9. Do I have an emotional support system?

9. Am I feeling disconnected from my emotional support system?

He who knows others is wise; he who knows himself is enlightened.

— Lao Tzu

Gaining Control of Ourselves

Then ask yourself:

1. What would help me feel more optimistic?

2. What would help me feel more encouraged?

3. Which beliefs can I change?

4. What can I find to appreciate?

5. What can I find to be thankful for?

6. What would help me feel more connected to others?

7. What would help me be less dependent on them?

8. What can I do to strengthen my emotional support system?

9. What small goal could I achieve *right now* that I am sure I can do?

> *Nothing can stop the man with the right mental attitude from achieving his goal; nothing on earth can help the man with the wrong mental attitude*
>
> *– W. W. Ziege*

Gaining Control of Ourselves

Anger

The real test of our ability to understand, respond to, and manage our emotions is the way we handle anger.

- Do we use it in productive or counter-productive ways?
- Does our anger lengthen or shorten our lives?

There are several important things to remember when speaking of anger:

1. It is a powerful survival tool.
2. It is a source of energy.
3. It is a secondary emotion.
4. When angry, our brain "downshifts."
5. Our thoughts are revolving at a more rapid rate.
6. Anger that lasts for a long time is harmful.
7. Anger held in is also very unhealthy.
8. Everyone gets angry.

NEVER RUIN AN APOLOGY WITH AN EXCUSE.
-KIMBERLY JOHNSON

Gaining Control of Ourselves

Anger is an energizer

Anger is a natural emotional state and is designed to help us stay alive. Anger sends signals to all parts of our body to help us fight. It energizes us and prepares us for action. Often, the perceived need to protect oneself comes from what amounts to psychological attacks from others.

Use anger wisely

When we feel energized by anger, it is smart to ask ourselves how we put this energy to its most productive use. As with the use of other forms of energy such as electricity, we want to use it efficiently, not wastefully.

Anger is secondary

One of the most helpful things to remember about anger is that it is a secondary emotion. A primary feeling is what is felt immediately before we feel angry. *We always feel something else first, even if we don't notice it.* We might feel afraid, attacked, offended, disrespected, forced, controlled, trapped, interrogated, or pressured. If any of these feelings are intense enough, they can lead to anger before we realize what we really felt!

Identify the primary emotion

An important point to remember about secondary feelings such as anger is that they do not identify the unmet emotional need. When all you can say is *"I feel angry,"* neither you nor any one else knows what would help you feel better. An amazingly simple, but effective technique is to always identify the primary emotion.

Situations that cause anger can be avoided

Here is an example. Assume someone wants us to do something we prefer not to do. At first we feel a little pressured but not enough to get angry. When they keep pushing us, we begin to get irritated. If they continue, we become "angry".

Communicate your feelings

An effective way to avoid getting angry in many cases is simply to express your feeling before it has been elevated to the point of anger. The *"I" Statements* of Assertive Communication, in the next chapter, are a good way to do this. This helps keep the brain in balance and out of the more volatile mode where it has downshifted to a more primitive and physiological response.

Gaining Control of Ourselves

Anger as a Response to Fear

One of the primitive functions of an animal's response to fear is to frighten away the attacker. We still experience anger as a response to fear but we are often unaware of this connection. According to Researchers from UCLA and the Rand Corporation, the attacks of 9/11 created unprecedented fear, anxiety and grief, which quickly lead to stress and anger. In modern human life, we often frighten away those who we need and care about most. **The most common recipients of our anger are persons who are closest to us.** Prolonged anger has clear health consequences. These include heart attacks, hardening of the arteries, strokes, hypertension, high blood pressure, heart rate and metabolic changes, muscle, and respiratory problems. People who are frequently angry have seven times the death rate of those who are more calm.

Responding to and Learning from Anger

Anger is an intense emotion. It shows that we feel strongly about something. As with every emotion, it has a **lesson** for us. It can teach us what we value, what we need, what we lack, what we believe and what our insecurities are. *It can help us become more aware of what we feel strongly about and which emotional needs are important to us.* One way to learn from anger is shown in the example below:

Instead of saying:

She never should have done that. I can't believe how irresponsible, insensitive, and inconsiderate she is. What a cold-hearted, evil bitch she is.

Take a timeout and ask yourself a couple of questions before you explode.

Consider saying to yourself:

I am really upset by this.
Why does it bother me so much?
What specifically am I feeling?
What are my primary feelings?
What need do I have that is not being met?
What principles of mine have been violated?

Gaining Control of Ourselves

Options are always available

From the answers to these questions, you can decide what course of action to take in view of what your goals are. *Simply being aware that you have many options and that you can decide to pick the best one helps reduce the anger.* It may help; for instance, to ask if you really want to frighten away the person you are angry with. As soon as you *"up-shift,"* begin to think about your options and their consequences, and make appropriate plans, you will begin to feel more in control and less threatened.

Use your anger productively

Remember that there is a space between stimulus and response and in this space lies your power to choose the option that is in your long-term best interest. Simply remembering that you have a choice will help you feel more in control. Not surprisingly, studies show that people feel better and are healthier when they have a sense of control over their lives. This is where the balance between upper brain and lower brain comes in. High emotional intelligence suggests that we channel our anger in productive ways to help us achieve our goals rather than to sabotage them. Keeping our goals clearly in mind at all times helps us accomplish this.

Here are some suggestions for responding to your anger:
- Ask what you are afraid of.
- Ask what feelings preceded the anger.
- Ask what other feelings you are having.
- Ask what you are trying to control.
- Ask what you can control.
- Consider your options.
- Choose the option that will bring you the most long-term happiness.

Control your anger before it controls you

Finally, if you practice catching your anger early on, before it escalates to the point where you begin to feel "ticked-off," you can ask yourself: "How can I best channel my energy so that I feel good about myself?" It is a simple little technique, but it makes a big difference in how you respond.

The place to improve the world is first in one's own heart and hands, and then work outward from there.

– Robert M. Pirsig

Gaining Control of Ourselves

> *Anger Management*
>
> According to *Six Seconds*, the leading emotional intelligence organization in the nation:
>
> - *It takes six seconds to manage anger*
> - *It takes six seconds to create compassion*
> - *It takes six seconds to make a difference*

While it will take longer to make permanent changes in your interactions with others, the first steps can and should be taken in an environment that supports change and growth. Such an environment is a class designed to teach skills in managing anger.

Some Reasons For Anger

- Making excessively high demands.
- Overstepping the bounds of one's authority.
- Insulting the other party.
- Causing the other party to lose face.
- Showing personal animosity toward another in a professional relationship.
- Falsely accusing the other party of wrongdoing.
- Failing to honor agreements, both formal and informal.
- Failing to reciprocate the other party's concessions.
- Failing to adequately prepare and/or organize for negotiation.
- Lacking real commitment to achieving an agreement or making it work.
- Questioning a person's authority or intentions.
- Seeking ways to undermine someone's authority by "going over his or her head."
- Showing excessive concern for unimportant details without viewing them in the larger context (the big picture).
- Invasion of personal space.
- Dissatisfaction.
- Non-recognition of needs.
- Disrespectful communication.
- Projection or externalization of anger at oneself.
- Desire for intimacy.
- Need for recognition or attention.
- Shame or humiliation.

Gaining Control of Ourselves

- Need to be heard.
- To cover a weakness or divert attention from a sensitive subject.
- Destruction of personal property.
- Do you have any other reasons for anger?

_____
_____
_____

Some Reasons To Give Up Anger

- Anger is a form of connection with someone you dislike.
- Anger injures both you and the person with whom you are communicating.
- Anger identifies the other as enemy and does not allow for empathy which leaves room for a better understanding of the other.
- Anger converts the self from victim to perpetrator.
- Anger is a reflection of a weakness, or vulnerability to others. Internal strength reduces the need to display anger, therefore, the actions of others need not bother you..

Recognizing Anger

Everyone gets angry. Anger is a *normal* emotion that everyone experiences at one time or another. Conflicts with others, not getting one's way, the inability to communicate, or overwhelming stress may cause anger. Everyone experiences feelings of anger, but open displays of anger are socially inappropriate and discouraged in society. When anger gets out of control and turns destructive, it can lead to problems: problems at work, in your personal relationships, and in the overall quality of your life. It can make you feel as though you're at the mercy of an unpredictable and powerful emotion.

Gaining Control of Ourselves

Anger a problem?

Whether or not anger is a problem for you depends on the consequences or outcome of your anger. Are there hurtful or harmful consequences to others as a result of your anger? Do you do hurtful things to yourself or others as a result of your anger? All too often anger turns into violent outbursts. Violence, as an expression of anger, has a long list of negative consequences. It may mean losing a relationship or being arrested, or being sent to the principal's office, or suspended, and it definitely means not feeling good about yourself afterward. Anger, in and of itself, is not the problem. However, **uncontrollable anger**, which leads to **aggression**, is the **harmful behavior** that **must be stopped**.

Communicate to reduce anger

Developing a pattern of internalizing–not expressing–your anger may actually lead to explosive outbursts of violence ("*pressure-cooker effect*"). Unexpressed anger can create other problems. It can lead to unhealthy expressions of anger, such as passive-aggressive behavior (getting back at people indirectly, without telling them why, rather than confronting them head-on) or appearing hostile and cynical. People who are constantly putting others down, criticizing everything and making cynical comments haven't learned how to constructively express their anger. Not surprisingly, those people aren't likely to have many successful relationships. Internalized anger raises blood pressure higher than actively expressed anger!

Hence, as angry feelings present themselves, they should be expressed *assertively* in a direct, non-intimidating manner. Otherwise, unresolved anger will grow and develop in its intensity, frequently leading to explosiveness.

Make the correct choice

Our goal is to help you understand your anger better and lessen the chances of your angry outbursts. The best way to begin is by becoming more aware of your expressions of anger. One of the advantages of being human is that we do not have to be victims of our environment or circumstance. We have the kind of intelligence that allows us to be in control of our responses, by making appropriate choices.

It's not the event but how it is interpreted

In many ways, anger is like stress–in order for it to be managed, it must first be recognized. Your reaction to anger-provoking situations must also be recognized. To understand how anger works, remember that events have no emotional value–it is how we interpret and respond that determines the outcome. The process of our *appraisal* gives meaning to the situation or event. Depending on the intensity of

Gaining Control of Ourselves

the appraisal, we may experience a change in our bodies relative to preparing for an attack. This occurs when we appraise a situation in an angry manner. This preparation can lead to angry actions. If we can learn these signals, we can immediately act to slow the process down and determine the most appropriate response. Here are some ways we express anger:

Anger Turned Outward	**Anger Turned Inward**
Verbalization of anger	Feeling upset
Irritation	Substance abuse
Swearing	Unhappiness
Hostility	Feeling hurt
Contempt	Guilt
Clenched fists	Feeling inferior
Insulting remarks	Low self-esteem
Intimidation	Sense of failure
Bragging about violent acts	Humiliation
Provoking behaviors	Feeling harassed
Sadistic acts	Envy
Verbal abuse	Feeling violated
Temper tantrums	Feeling alienated
Violation of others' rights	Feeling depressed
Screaming	Powerless feelings
Defiance	Helpless
Rage	Apathy
Cruel teasing	Feeling out of control
Excessively argumentative	Feeling rejected
Threats	Words as weapons
Damage to property	Resentment
Assault	Bitterness
Domination	Irrationality
Annoyance	Rigidity
Impatience	Biting sarcasm
Frustration	
Tense facial expression	

Gaining Control of Ourselves

NOTES:

Gaining Control of Ourselves

Identifying High-Risk Situations

There are a number of "high-risk" situations, which may make you vulnerable to angry or violent behavior. It may be helpful for you to review the following list of commonly identified factors to determine if any of these pose a threat to your continued growth. Once you identify your possible high-risk factors, you can then begin to plan prevention strategies to help you handle these without explosive anger. The best way of managing anger is to recognize the early warning signs and prevent the anger from becoming out of control. The following is a list of high-risk factors identified by other participants, research studies, and professional counselors or therapists:

Negative Feelings, Attitudes, Thoughts, or Behaviors:

Anger expression problems (*i.e.* holding anger in, expressing it inappropriately, or aggressively). Under each section, *circle the number next to the high-risk factor that applies to you:*

1. Anxiety or nervousness.
2. Boredom or lack of constructive leisure interests.
3. Denial – *"I am not angry!"*
4. Depression.
5. Excessive or impulsive behaviors, for example: gambling too much, overeating, spending too much money, or overworking.
6. Exhaustion or fatigue.

Gaining Control of Ourselves

7. Fears that seem unreasonable.
8. Feeling helpless or hopeless.
9. Guilt.
10. Impatience: things aren't happening fast enough.
11. Lack of meaning in life (nothing seems important, there is not much pleasure in your life).
12. Loneliness or isolating yourself from others.
13. Painful memories, for example: from combat experience, divorce, death of a loved one, or from experiences growing up in a troubled family.
14. Preoccupation with alcohol or drugs.
15. Resentment toward others.
16. Self-pity.
17. Shame.
18. Socializing with others in bars or using drugs.

Problems in Relationships with Other People

1. Incessant argumentativeness with others.
2. Difficulty meeting people or developing new relationships.
3. Difficulty trusting others.
4. Problems in meeting new friends.
5. Friends consist mainly of others who abuse alcohol or drugs.
6. Spouse or partner has an alcohol or drug problem.
7. Sexual problems, for example: impotence, lack of control over sexual feelings or behaviors, or inappropriate sexual behavior.
8. Specific stresses or problems in a relationship.
    - "I just can't seem to get along with my parents, children, or spouse."
    - "I can't seem to handle my responsibilities as a parent."
9. Other: _____
   _____
   _____

Gaining Control of Ourselves

Other High-Risk Situations

1. Achieving success at my job (getting promoted).
2. Difficulty handling evenings or weekends.
3. Difficulty solving problems without feeling overwhelmed.
4. Feeling good and happy about myself and my life.
5. Lack of constructive ways to spend my days.
6. Lack of hobbies or leisure time interests.
7. Physical pain or problems.
8. Other: _____
   _____
   _____

To say "yes," you have to sweat and roll up your sleeves and plunge both hands into life up to the elbows. It is easy to say "no."

- *Jean Anouilh*

Anger is a defensive emotion. It teaches us to "No it all," denying our family, friends, and co-workers simple favors we could easily grant. All too often we say "no" automatically; it is our default response.

This doesn't have to be. We can learn to say "yes." Learning to say yes affirms our connection to others, affirms our positive intent, and helps us avoid slipping into anger automatically.

Each day, find a situation in which you can say "yes" without violating your own boundaries, without being submissive, without losing integrity. Practice saying "yes" with a passion for life and compassion for others. The results of this simple exercise may surprise you as you find your relationships improving along with your mood and feelings about yourself.

Gaining Control of Ourselves

The Anger Log

When we look at the situations that make us angry, it is common to blame situations and other people for our anger. We tend to think what other people do, or what happens to us, causes our anger. However, contrary to the belief that other people or situations make us angry, *what really makes us angry is thinking angrily about the things that happen to us*. What we think or tell ourselves about an event makes us angry, not the event itself.

We feel the way we think

When we judge or evaluate something as negative, we usually become upset. If we judge or evaluate something more positively, we will usually feel better. Basically, we are not upset by things, but by our thinking about the situation. In other words, we feel the way we think. Angry thoughts lead to angry feelings. There are many ways to get our points across without becoming aggressive or violent. Non-violent ways of communicating will influence people to react in a reciprocal manner.

This section can help you understand your anger and lessen the chances of angry outbursts or violence. The best way to begin is by becoming more aware of the triggering thoughts and consequences of anger. You can do this by keeping an *Anger Log*.

Writing it down helps

During the next few days, whenever you are aware of feeling angry, describe the situation about which you feel angry by writing in the space labeled "Situation". Also, describe under "Actions" what you did as a result of getting angry. You may fill out your Anger Log immediately after the situation or at the end of the day when you reflect on your day's events. You don't even need to use the pages in this workbook, you can write on any paper—simply include the date, a brief (three line) description of the event, and the ABCD sections.

Situation: Describe the situation about which you became angry.

- A. ***Beliefs*** – What did you tell yourself about the situation?
- B. ***Feelings*** – Describe how you felt.
- C. ***Actions*** – Describe what you did.
- D. ***Dispute*** – If your thinking is what caused the anger, modify your thought processes.

Gaining Control of Ourselves

New self-messages can make the difference

You can change your feelings by questioning your angry thoughts. At the "D" step in the *ABCD* format, we start the process of sending ourselves some new self-messages to take the place of our *self-centered*, demanding thinking. These kinds of new, helpful self-messages are more realistic and less upsetting and can help us reduce our anger and our need to control.

- Who said so?
- Why?
- Where is my evidence?
- Is there a more helpful way of looking at the situation?

Using the ABCD format as a personal inventory helps us get a clearer picture of the factors contributing to our anger. We can gradually observe the changes as a result of this process. After reading the following examples demonstrating the ABCD process, write three of your own examples.

Example 1:

Situation: About what did you become angry?
   I am in a restaurant and have to wait a long time to be waited on by the server.

A: Beliefs – What did you think or tell yourself about the situation?
   The server is a bitch because she keeps me waiting. I hate waiting in line for anything. It is awful that I have to wait so long.

B: Feelings – Your feelings following the situation.
   I felt angry.

C: Action – What you did because of your anger.
   I criticized the server in a very angry manner. The server left crying.

D: Dispute – Other ways of looking at the situation.
   I had to wait a long time to be served because it was really busy at the restaurant. The server was doing a good job, considering that she was working alone.

Gaining Control of Ourselves

Example 2:

Situation: I am driving behind someone going 30 in a 50 MPH speed zone, and I'm late for an appointment.

A: Beliefs – *This person is a real idiot. He should drive according to the speed limit. He shouldn't hold me up. I have to get to my appointment on time.*

B: Feelings – *Frustrated, pissed. Anger level 6 on a 1-10 scale. Primary emotions: anxiety and frustration.*

C: Action – *Tailgate, honk, and make finger gestures.*

D: Dispute – *Who said he should drive fifty miles per hour? I said so. There is no reason I should try and control others. Why do I have to get to this appointment on time? It won't be the end of the world if I'm late. I can stop being so demanding. Maybe the person is driving as fast as he safely can. It would be best for me to wait and pass him when it's safe. Perhaps I need to learn to drive defensively.*

Example 3:

Situation: My partner has revealed a personal and embarassing intimacy about me at a party.

E: Beliefs – *He/she must really hate me. What a vicious hit below the belt!*

F: Feelings – *Furious, silently enraged and resentful. Anger level 8 on a 1-10 scale. Primary emotions: humiliation and embarassment.*

G: Action – *Avoid partner during party, silent treatment on drive home, snide comments.*

H: Dispute – *That really hurt me. Could it have been on purpose? Maybe he/she didn't mean any harm.*

The important thing...is not so much to obtain new facts as to discover new ways of thinking about them.

- Sir William Lawrence Bragg

Gaining Control of Ourselves

NOTES:

Gaining Control of Ourselves

Your Own Anger Log

It is important that participants keep a Weekly *Anger Log* because it will help you get the full benefit of this class. You should have at least one entry a week, better yet, one each day. You can describe anger with your wife, parents, children, teacher, friends, or others. The purpose is to practice identifying when you feel angry and replacing anger producing thoughts.

Step 1:

Date: ____/____/____

Situation: _____
_____
_____

A. Beliefs: _____
_____
_____

B. Feelings: _____
_____
_____

C. Action: _____
_____
_____

D. Dispute: _____
_____
_____

Gaining Control of Ourselves

Date: ____/____/____

Situation: _____

_____

_____

A. Beliefs: _____

_____

_____

B. Feelings: _____

_____

_____

C. Action: _____

_____

_____

D. Dispute: _____

_____

_____

Gaining Control of Ourselves

Date: ____/____/____

Situation: _____

_____

_____

A. Beliefs: _____

_____

_____

B. Feelings: _____

_____

_____

C. Action: _____

_____

_____

D. Dispute: _____

_____

_____

Gaining Control of Ourselves

Step 2:

With the *Anger Log* you completed on the previous page, please rate the intensity of your anger on a scale of 1 to 10 (1 being low-level anger, and 10 being high-level anger).

Not So Angry　　　　　　　　　**Anger Levels**　　　　　　　　　**Very Angry**

1	2	3	4	5	6	7	8	9	10
Bugged	*Bothered*	*Annoyed*	*Irritated*	*Agitated*	*Mad*	*Pissed-Off*	*Furious*	*Enraged*	*Exploding*

Comments:

_____

_____

Behavior Signs:

_____

_____

Situation:

_____

_____

Self-talk:

_____

_____

Did you take a time-out? Yes ❑　No ❑

Comments:

_____

_____

Did you avoid the situation and keep all of your anger inside?　　Yes ❑　No ❑

Comments:

_____

_____

Gaining Control of Ourselves

Did you focus your anger on someone or something? Yes ❑ No ❑

Comments:
_____
_____

How did you handle the situation?
_____
_____

Self-rating of your control afterwards:

1	2	3	4	5	6	7	8	9	10	11	12

Good Control   *No Control*

"I'm feeling better now. Not angry at all."

Gaining Control of Ourselves

Seven Steps to Anger Control

1. **Feelings:** Start with your upsetting feelings. Identify them. Use them as stop signs. Your upset feelings are signals that *you are telling yourself upsetting things*. You may have to become a better observer of your feelings. This means getting in touch with your feelings.

2. **Thoughts:** Identify the upsetting thoughts that are making you angry about the situation. What are you trying to control? Question your upsetting thoughts. Ask yourself "Why must I get my way?" "Why should others do what I want?" Then answer your questions.

3. **Reframe:** Counteract your upsetting thoughts with a positive self-message. Put the brakes on your feelings. Tell yourself, "Slow down, easy does it."

4. **Clarify:** Clarify the situation for yourself. Ask yourself, "What is really going on in the situation?" You can then feel disappointed with the situation but not enraged at the people who are creating it.

5. **Goals:** Set some more realistic goals for yourself in regard to the problem situation. Ask yourself, "What alternative solution can I use to resolve this situation?" Be specific and concrete. What can you do to change the situation?

6. **Options:** List the constructive options you have in order to reach your goals. Ask yourself, "What constructive actions can I take to reach my goals?"

7. **Action:** Choose a constructive option to reach your goal and act on it. The end result of the *ABCD* process is **POSITIVE ACTION** on your part.

If we could read the secret history of our enemies, we should find in each person's life sorrow and suffering enough to disarm any hostility.
      (anonymous)

Gaining Control of Ourselves

Taking a Time-Out

Anger is an escalating process. At its peak, our destructive self-statements and high level of anger arousal often lead to verbal and physical aggression. Almost all of us can remember a time when we took a swipe at someone or–if we didn't physically strike our opponent–we wounded him or her with verbal attacks.

Out of control

When anger gets this hot, it is almost impossible to act or think productively. That's because our thoughts, anger arousal, and behavior are moving each other toward an explosion, trapping us in our own anger. For most people, the rage tends to go away or reduce after time.

Start now!

The technique of taking a time-out will immediately help you de-escalate your anger before it becomes too intense. Since intense anger leads to verbal and physical abuse for so many people, and because of its adverse physical effects, begin using the time-out **right away**. That way, you can avoid the anger trap.

Steps to Take:

Stop & think about what you are doing

When you feel a situation is likely to trigger your anger, decide to take a "Time-Out." This means you temporarily remove yourself from the situation. Give yourself an opportunity to think through what is happening and try to think of a way of resolving the situation in a manner that doesn't lead to violent words or actions. A time-out is an excellent opportunity to make an anger log entry—in fact, making the entry may even help you to change your response to the situation!

Gaining Control of Ourselves

Keep the Volume down

Do not swear, raise your voice, threaten, or use any intimidating behavior. Go somewhere and try to relax and think positively about yourself. Remind yourself of your goals. It may help to walk, jog, or take a deep breath to relax. Do not drive, drink alcohol, or take drugs.

If at first you don't succeed

When you come back, decide if you can discuss the situation with whomever is the source of the disagreement. Sometimes after a time-out you may both decide that the issue was not worth discussing in the first place, and you may mutually decide to just drop it. If you decide to discuss the issue and you recognize the cues occurring again–**TAKE ANOTHER TIME-OUT!**

Practice, Practice, Practice

It's important that you practice time-outs so that you can more easily take the real time-outs. They appear to be the same, except that, in the practice time-out, you are not feeling angry.

Why Does a Time-Out Work?

- *I'm...*
  When you express your feelings with an "I" statement, it minimizes name-calling and blame.

- **... I am beginning to feel upset.**
  You are talking about how you feel. It's a direct communication, and there is nothing unclear about this statement.

- **... I need to take a time-out.**
  Another "I" statement. You are also saying to the listener that you are not going to lose control; instead, you're going to do something else, like take a time-out. Taking a time-out helps build trust with the other person–that there will be NO VIOLENCE.

Leave for an hour

If the disagreement is with an intimate partner and you stay away for a full hour, you and she/he should be sufficiently cooled off by the time you return. If you agree to come back in an hour, live up to your agreement – it helps to build trust.

Gaining Control of Ourselves

Don't drink or drive.

Drinking and abusing drugs will only make the situation worse. Don't drive – there are already enough angry people on the road! Plus, road rage may already be a problem for you.

Do something physical.

Going for a walk, a run, or a ride on your bicycle will help discharge some of the angry tension in your body.

Check in – talk about what it was that made you angry.

If you do no more than check in, you have completed the exercise. If you go on to talk about what it was that made you angry, you gain additional experience and practice in communicating and discussing emotional issues.

Time-Outs Are Hard To Do!

Why? Many men grow up believing that only cowards will walk away from a fight. Your impulse will be to stay and finish it, or at least to get in the last word. Is it more important to maintain your image as a "real man," or to stop the cycle of anger and aggression?

Many men have also expressed the fear that their partners will be gone when they return. This is part of *trust-building*. As each of you follow through with your part in taking a time-out, the trust will grow.

The other frequent problem men have with time-outs is staying away from alcohol. Many people use alcohol to treat loneliness, and you may feel quite alone during your time-out. Also, men will often go to a bar to hang out with their buddies when they need support or someone to talk to. We want to emphasize again that alcohol can make an argument much worse. **DON'T DRINK!!!**

When Taking a Time-Out,
These Are Some of the Things You Can Say To Yourself:

1. I don't need to prove myself in this situation. I can stay calm.
2. As long as I keep my cool, I'm in control of myself.
3. No need to doubt myself, what other people say doesn't matter.
4. I'm the only person who can make me mad or keep me calm.
5. I need to take time to relax and slow things down.

Gaining Control of Ourselves

6. My anger is a signal. Time to talk to myself and to relax.

7. I don't need to feel threatened here. I can relax and stay cool.

8. Nothing says I have to be competent and strong all the time.

9. It's okay to feel unsure or confused.

10. It is impossible to control other people and situations. The only thing I can control is myself and how I express my feelings.

11. It is okay to be uncertain or insecure sometimes. I don't need to be in control of everything and everybody.

12. If people criticize me, I can survive that. Nothing says I have to be perfect.

13. If this person wants to go off the wall, that's their thing.

14. I don't need to respond to their anger or feel threatened.

15. When I get into an argument, I can take a time-out.

16. Most things people argue about are stupid and insignificant. I can recognize that my anger comes from old feelings. It's okay to walk away from this fight.

Strategies to Handle High-Risk Situations

Choose two high-risk situations that could lead to anger for you. Review all the facts. After you carefully review the list of high-risk factors, go back over the ones you marked related to each of these.

For each of the two high-risk situations you identified, write in below the situation and information and three coping strategies or ways you can handle these without resorting to explosive behaviors.

Nobody has a right to sit down and feel helpless. There's too much to do!

- Dorothy Day

Gaining Control of Ourselves

High-Risk Situation 1: Situation and related information

_____
_____
_____
_____

Coping Strategy 1: _____
Coping Strategy 2: _____
Coping Strategy 3: _____

High-Risk Situation 2: Situation and related information

_____
_____
_____
_____

Coping Strategy 1: _____
Coping Strategy 2: _____
Coping Strategy 3: _____

Gaining Control of Ourselves

Review

1. Describe what the *ABCD* format in anger management stands for and give a personal example of a situation in which you were angry:

A:
_____
_____
_____

B:
_____
_____
_____

C:
_____
_____
_____

D:
_____
_____
_____

2. List three of the seven steps that we can use to control anger.

   1. _____
   2. _____
   3. _____

3. List three skills you have learned in stress management.

   1. _____
   2. _____
   3. _____

Gaining Control of Ourselves

NOTES:

Part 4: Communication

Improving Communication with Others

Lack of communication is the root of many troubles, such as hurt feelings, misunderstandings, missed deadlines, and unsuccessful connections. Healthy communication in its broadest form is important in developing positive healthy relationships between family members and others. Skills for acquiring good communication techniques are emphasized in this section.

Basic skills are very important and many people do not use them well. Poor communication skills result in unnecessary problems and misunderstandings in relationships.

Good communication requires two sets of skills:

- Those required to understand the other person (*accurate receiving*).
- Those required to give out accurate messages (*accurate sending*).

Four key communication skills for improving interpersonal relations are:

- The ability to listen without judging.
- Show understanding of what has been said.
- Acknowledge and accept another's point of view.
- Don't impose your personal beliefs on someone else.

Good communication skills take patience and time to acquire. We encourage participants to use all of their newly learned skills in developing positive healthy relationships.

> The aim of an argument or discussion should not be victory, but progress.
>
> - Joseph Joubert

Gaining Control of Ourselves

Self–Assessment:
Understanding and Dealing with Feelings

Emotional maturity is essential to the growth process. In the following exercise we will explore where we are and where we are going in relation to our feelings. This is a very important component in the process of improving communication as well as increasing emotional intelligence.

1. List at least three feelings you have a hard time identifying in yourself:

2. What is one feeling you have difficulty communicating to others?

3. List some feelings you find easy to identify and communicate:

4. What do you want to change in the way you deal with your feelings?

5. What do you see as a good communication skill that helps you express your feelings?

6. Of the skills for successful communication and intimacy listed on the following page, which do you have and which do you need to develop? Place a check in the appropriate column.

Gaining Control of Ourselves

Skill	Have This	Need to Develop
Ability to listen to others		
Ability to state needs clearly		
Ability to see choices		
Ability to compromise		
Ability to respect another's opinion		
Ability to share feelings		
Ability to accept outside help		
Ability to admit mistakes		
Ability to appreciate and nurture others		
Ability to value yourself		
Patience		
Courage		
Honesty		
Others:		

> **TACT IS THE KNACK OF MAKING A POINT WITHOUT MAKING AN ENEMY.**
>
> **-SIR ISAAC NEWTON**

Gaining Control of Ourselves

Open Communication

Roadblocks to Open Communication

Commanding: (The general)
Telling someone to do something, giving him or her an order or a command.

Threatening: (The principal)
Telling someone how you will punish him or her if he or she does or does not do something.

Moralizing: (The preacher)
Quoting rules or authority as accepted truth.

Advising:
Offering solutions to others because you think you know best. Telling someone how to solve a problem, giving him or her advice or suggestions, providing solutions for him or her (when he/she did not ask for advice).

Using Logical Arguments: (The teacher)
Trying to convince the other person with facts, counter-arguments, logic, information, or your opinions.

Judging, Criticizing, Disagreeing, Blaming: (The judge)
Making a negative judgment or evaluation of the other person.

Name-Calling, Labeling, Stereotyping: (The librarian)

Title of Group HEALTHY REL. (eff. comm)

Facilitator of Group _____

What did you learn from the topic? Learned that open ones to listen, pay attention to my peers more.

What was your mood during group? I'm in a neutral good mood.

GIVE YOUR OPINION OF GROUP

Name: CRYSTAL WHITE

Date of Group 02.29.20

Time of Group 1:00 (1:50)

Gaining Control of Ourselves

Putting the other person into a category, usually negative ("*You are never going to change.*").

Interpreting, Analyzing, Diagnosing: (The shrink)
Telling the other person what his motives are or analyzing what he or she is doing or saying; communicating that you have him or her figured out and diagnosed.

Denying the Importance of Another's Feelings: (The movie star)
Trying to "make" the other person believe that their feelings are not important. Telling the other person that you know how they feel.

Probing, Questioning, Interrogating, Cross-Examining: (The lawyer)
Trying to find reasons, motives, and/or causes, rather than focusing on what the other person wants to say (one person, the questioner, determines the course of the conversation).

Withdrawing, Distracting, Using Sarcasm, Humoring, Diverting: (The comedian)
Trying to move the other away from the problem; withdrawing from the problem yourself; pushing the problem aside by changing the topic. Avoidance.

Phrases for Miscommunication

Ordering...	"*You must... You have to... You will..*"
Threatening...	"*If you don't, then... You'd better, or else...*"
Preaching...	"*You should... You ought... It's your duty...*"
Lecturing...	"*Here is where you're wrong... Do you realize...*"
Giving Answers...	"*What I would do is... it would be best if you...*"
Judging...	"*You are argumentative. Lazy. You'll never change.*"
Excusing...	"*It's not so bad... You'll feel better...*"
Diagnosing...	"*You're just trying to get attention... What you need is...*"
Interrogation...	"*When? How? What? Where? Who?*"
Labeling...	"*You're being unrealistic... emotional... angry...*"
Manipulating...	"*Don't you think you should...?*"

> Selfishness is not living as one wishes to live, it is asking others to live as one wishes to live.
> -Oscar Wilde

Gaining Control of Ourselves

Positive Communication Skills

Silence, Passive Listening:

Listening to another person's message without verbally replying.
Silence can be a powerful "non-verbal" message–communicating acceptance. Sometimes all another person needs from you is to be heard. This is something that can be accomplished by simply "listening." Passive listening communicates acceptance to the other person if the listener gives undivided attention so the speaker knows that he is being heard.

Listening with your heart means trying to determine how the other person is feeling as they are speaking. This is empathy.

Simple Acknowledgement:

Verbal communicative responses to another's message.
These responses convey the idea that you are listening. Such messages or expressions as:

- "Oh."
- "I see."
- "Un-hummm."
- "Really?"
- "Interesting."
- "No fooling?"

These signals let the other person know that you are listening and "tuned in" but offer no content, evaluation or judgment. Your responses simply allow the speaker to proceed with the message.

Door Openers:

Verbal responses which are invitations to say more.
Responses such as: "I'd like to hear about that," "Would you like to talk about it?" "Tell me about it," and "Sounds like you have some strong feelings about this," are ways you can communicate your willingness to continue listening. These types of statements encourage people to begin to talk, or continue talking. Such statements "keep the ball with the other person" by leaving your feelings and thoughts out of the communication. Door openers convey acceptance of the other person by communicating, in effect, "I respect you as a person with the right to express yourself," "I really want to hear your point of view," and, "I am interested in you."

Gaining Control of Ourselves

Active Listening:

Messages that convey back to the sender empathic understanding of her communications.

Active listening is the process of "decoding" the words a person uses to express an idea or feeling and "feeding back" to the sender her decoded message for verification.

Send the right message

In Active Listening the receiver does not send a message of his own, such as evaluation, logic, advice, analysis, or questions. He feeds back only what he thinks the sender's message meant, *nothing more or less*. Active listening does not include "interrogation" or questioning. The listener only asks questions to clarify what he or she is unsure of.

People will connect with a person who is an Active Listener

Active listening helps people free themselves of troublesome feelings by encouraging the free expression of these feelings. It helps people become less afraid of feelings. When you accept a person's feelings, she hears that her feelings are not "bad." Active listening promotes a relationship of warmth between you and the other person. A person who experiences being heard will feel close to you and you in turn will feel warm and close to the other person.

Examples of some Active Listening Responses

...VALIDATE the speaker:

Show the speaker you care about him or her. Say how glad you are he or she is talking with you

    Speaker: "I'm having some problems at work."
    Listener: "I'm glad you feel comfortable talking to me about it."

...ENCOURAGE the speaker:

Show the speaker you want him or her to continue talking. Say things so the speaker knows you are interested in what she or he is saying:

    Speaker: "I'm having some problems with my employer."
    Listener: "Can you tell me more about it?"

...POSE OPEN-ENDED QUESTIONS to the speaker:

Show the speaker you want to understand what he or she is saying. Ask questions to get more information from the speaker:

    Speaker: "I can't stand my job anymore."

Gaining Control of Ourselves

Listener: "What don't you like about the job?"

...RESTATE back to the speaker:
Show the speaker you understand the importance of what she or he is saying. Say what the speaker said *in your own words*:
Speaker: "My employer is not giving me the recognition I deserve at work."
Listener: "It seems like your employer is not valuing you as an important worker."

...REFLECT back to the speaker:
Show the speaker you understand what he or she is feeling. Respond to the speaker with a "feeling word" in your statement:
Speaker: "I want to quit my job but I cannot afford to do that."
Listener: "It sounds like you might feel trapped."

...SUMMARIZE what the speaker said:
Show the speaker you can pull together all the things he or she has said. Help the speaker move onto the next idea or issue:
Speaker: "I am having a lot of problems at work and I want to quit."
Listener: "Your job seems overwhelming and you wonder if it's the place for you anymore."

Phrases For Active Listening

Encouraging...	*"Can you tell me more?"*
Clarifying...	*"When did this happen?"*
Summarizing...	*"Let me see if I understand what you just said..."*
Acknowledging...	*"It sounds like you are very angry right now."*
Open Questioning...	*"What would you like to see happen?"*
Responding...	*"I see it this way... How do you see it?"*
Problem solving...	*"How would you resolve this issue?"*
Empathizing...	*"That sounds painful."*
Normalizing...	*"Many people feel the way you do..."*
Rephrasing...	*"I hear that you feel _____ when s/he _____ because..."*
Validating...	*"I am glad you feel comfortable talking to me about this."*

Gaining Control of Ourselves

Styles of Communication

There are four major styles of communication. Most of us use different styles of communication depending on the situation, our moods, and the behavior of the person with whom we are attempting to communicate.

Passive Communication:
The passive communicator avoids direct eye contact, fails to accurately express his or her feelings, and tends to have low self-esteem. His anger is self-directed rather than to the source of the anger.

Passive-Aggressive Communication:
The passive-aggressive communicator often sounds passive but is hostile in his manner of speaking. He often uses sarcasm and other hostile gestures to get his point across. The listener is left without any indication of what the passive-aggressive communicator needs or wants.

Aggressive Communication:
The aggressive communicator invades the space of the listener, speaks in a threatening manner, and may throw objects, glare or attempt to intimidate the listener. He or she often attempts to blame the listener for whatever the source of the disagreement may be.

Assertive Communication:
The assertive communicator speaks in a reasonable tone, establishes eye contact with the listener, uses "I messages", and clearly states his or her needs, feelings and requests. He invites the listener to work towards a mutually satisfactory resolution of the conflict. He consciously influences the listener by his own behavior. He demonstrates skills in emotional intelligence.

Defining myself, as opposed to being defined by others, is one of the most difficult challenges I face.

- Carol Mosely-Braun

Gaining Control of Ourselves

"I" Messages: Taking Responsibility for What You Feel

Using "I" messages is a way to take responsibility and control of your own feelings. To formulate an "I" message ask yourself:

I Feel*	How do you feel about the behavior?
When	What specifically is the behavior that bothers you?
Because	How does the behavior affect you?
I need	What would you like the other person to do differently?

* Note: Make sure to state a feeling or an emotion here. A statement like "I feel **that** …" disguises a **judgment** and is *not* a feeling. The next word after "I feel" **must be** a *feeling* like "mad," "sad," "hurt," "afraid," "frustrated," etc.

Example: An employee complains because her supervisor rarely tells him he's doing a good job. The employee might say:

I feel	*angry and hurt.*
When	*I am not complimented on my work.*
Because	*I don't think I'm a valuable employee.*
I need	*you to recognize my contributions to the unit.*

Example: A wife complains that her husband leaves the toilet seat up. She might say:

I feel	*frustrated.*
When	*you don't put the toilet seat down.*
Because	*I don't like sitting* IN *the toilet when it's dark.*
I need	*for you to put the seat down each time you use the bathroom.*

I never learned from a man who agreed with me.

-Robert Anson Heinlein

Gaining Control of Ourselves

Please fill in the blanks below to practice using "I" messages as a way of communicating your thoughts.

1. You're at a party. Your partner had a little too much to drink. She/he wants to drive you home.

    I feel _____

    When _____

    Because _____

    I need _____

2. You've told your son you want him to keep his room clean. You walk into the room and it is a total mess.

    I feel _____

    When _____

    Because _____

    I need _____

3. A car is parked in your assigned stall in your office parking lot. The driver is a co-worker who has done this before.

    I feel _____

    When _____

    Because _____

    I need _____

Guidelines to Resolving Conflicts with Intimate Partners

- Fight by mutual consent.
- Stick to the subject.
- Don't hit below the belt.
- Don't quit; work at it.
- Don't try to win, **EVER!**
- Respect crying.

*Remember, we tend to be enraged by people or situations that are important to us. We seldom become angry with others over situations that are not important to us. It's imperative to note that married partners have the purpose of clearing the air and expressing deep feelings in order to build a more unified life. Keep your goal in mind – **the goal of sharing your lives with each other**.*

Gaining Control of Ourselves

Words • Words • Words...

☹ "NO-NO" WORDS   ☺ "YES" WORDS

☹ "You never…"   ☺ "I'm sorry."

☹ "You always…"   ☺ "I need you."

☹ "I told you so…"   ☺ "Please help me."

☹ "I don't want to discuss it…"   ☺ "I did wrong…"

☹ "When will you ever learn?"   ☺ "Thank you."

☹ "How many times do I have to tell you?"   ☺ "I love you."

☺ "Help me understand …"

"Always" and "never" are two words you should always remember never to use.

– Wendell Johnson

When we use absolute words like "always" and "never," we create distance between ourselves and our partners. These words are judgmental, and generally an exaggeration that does more to hurt than to heal. They also disguise the **true** intent of our conversation. When I say "*You always squeeze the toothpaste in the middle,*" I actually mean to communicate "*I don't like it when you squeeze the toothpaste in the middle.*" When I say "*You never make the bed,*" I actually mean to communicate "*I would like you to make the bed.*" Using more honest language to express your true intent replaces judgmental language, and draws people closer together instead of pushing them apart.

Gaining Control of Ourselves

What Is Open For Negotiation In Intimate Relationships?

An issue is open for negotiation if it is not entirely one person's right to decide. An issue is open for discussion, but not negotiation if it is only one person's right to decide. If you think an item should be open for negotiation, put a check sign under 1 - Open. If you think it is open for discussion and input but not negotiation, because your partner has the right to make the decision, put a check sign under 2 - Not Open. If you think it is open for discussion and input but not negotiation, because it is your right to make the decision, put a check sign under 3 - Not Open.

Situation	1: Open	2: Not Open, Their Decision	3: Not Open, My Decision
1. Which friends s/he can spend time with?			
2. Which friends you can spend time with?			
3. Who cooks/cleans on the weekdays?			
4. Who cooks/cleans on the weekend?			
5. Will s/he drink or use drugs again?			
6. Will you drink/use drugs again?			
7. Will s/he drink on certain occasions?			
8. Will you drink on certain occasions?			
9. Who finds a sitter for the children?			

Gaining Control of Ourselves

Situation	1: Open	2: Not Open, Their Decision	3: Not Open, My Decision
10. Will s/he buy a car/truck with his/her own money?			
11. Will s/he get a job or change jobs?			
12. Will you get a job or change jobs?			
13. Will s/he go to school?			
14. Will you go to school?			
15. Which guests or relatives can visit your home?			
16. How will the children be disciplined?			
17. When will the children be disciplined?			
18. Can s/he go on a trip without you?			
19. Can you go on a trip without him/her?			
20. What is your paycheck spent on?			
21. What is his/her paycheck spent on?			

Remember These Four Points About Respectful Communication and Conflict Resolution

1. You have the right to say what you want to say, but you cannot do it in an abusive way, using intimidation or harsh language.

2. In order for communication to be effective, both parties must listen to what the other person is saying and not try to merely convince the other of their own position.

3. Good communication requires negotiation and compromise. If somebody has to win the argument, then somebody else has to lose it, and you've lost good communication.

4. No single issue is as important as your overall goal of remaining non-aggressive and non-evasive in your relationship.

 The most prfoundly creative way to overcome enemies is to make them our friends.

But this involves a series of painful acts: A constant decision never to achieve our goals by destroying or humiliating others.

-Dom Paulo Cardinal Arns

Gaining Control of Ourselves

Quiz:

Improving Communication

List and explain three elements of honest communication that you have learned:
-
-
-

List and explain three steps you can take in order to "cool down" and take a "Time Out:"
-
-
-

List two steps you can take to let go and lessen the negative or hurtful feelings:
-
-

I cannot love all humanity except with a vast and somewhat abstract love. But I love a few men, living or dead, with such force and admiration that I am always eager to preserve in others what will someday perhaps make them resemble those I love.

- Albert Camus

Gaining Control of Ourselves

Action Plan

DATE ____/____/____

Changes I Am Making	Specific Steps
☺	
☺	
☺	
☺	
☺	
☺	
☺	

Gaining Control of Ourselves

NOTES:

Gaining Control of Ourselves

Part 5: Role Modeling

Communication by Example

Setting a good example for your children is the most powerful way to teach them positive behaviors and attitudes. Parents who behave in a negative manner (fight constantly, abuse alcohol and/or drugs, are disrespectful, are unmotivated, etc.) teach their children to behave these ways. Parents who communicate with "do as I say, not as I do" confuse their children and harm their own credibility as parents. Hence, it is important that parents keep their actions and words consistent.

Someone is watching

One of the most powerful ways children learn is by watching their parents' actions. Today, it is widely recognized that children who were abused or grew up in homes with drug or alcohol use, may face emotional roadblocks as they develop. Such children experience an extremely negative example of family life.

What kind of messages are you sending?

Children can also be damaged by behavior that does not seem to be harmful. For instance, parents with low motivation or who deny responsibility for their failures may convey the message to their children that hard work, determination, and personal responsibility are not important. Like their parents, such children are likely to do poorly in school and may later have difficulty finding or staying with a career. When they do find a job, it may be in an occupation that is considerably less challenging and likely to be in the lower income levels.

Home environment counts

Through lack of interest and attention, parents tell their child that he or she is not important, has little value, and may not be worthy of love. Children growing up in such a family are likely to have low self-esteem and feelings of inadequacy. Such an environment sets the stage for difficulties and failures in school and other areas of life.

* * *

Children need models rather than critics.
-Joseph Joubert

Gaining Control of Ourselves

Negative Parental Examples and the Values they Communicate

Parental Example	Value Communicated
Adult lying	Adults cannot be trusted
Domestic violence and child abuse	The world is unsafe
Child neglect	Children are not valued, respected, loved
Constant family fighting	Life is not joyful/life is difficult
Constant emotional problems	Life is always difficult
Lack of parental integrity or morals	Honesty & respect for the law are not valued
Parental depression and lack of motivation	Pessimism and negativity are the norm

Positive Parental Examples And The Values They Communicate

Parental Example	Value Communicated
Working together as a family	Cooperation
Discussing news events/voting	Citizenship
Telling the truth	Honesty
Working hard at one's job	Work ethic
Keeping the house clean/being on time	Responsibility
Facing up to problems/challenges	Courage
Saying no to drugs/alcohol	Self-control, self-respect
Reading	Education
Helping less fortunate individuals	Compassion
Caring for your children	Love

These are just a few examples of the values communicated by negative and positive parental behaviors. When parents are aware that their behavior acts as a model for their children, they can take advantage of this powerful means of communication to reinforce the most important values. This awareness also helps parents make better decisions about which behaviors are appropriate in their role as parents.

Gaining Control of Ourselves

Quiz

1. Who was allowed to get angry in your childhood home? How did they express their anger?

2. What values did your parents instill in you as you were growing up?

3. What values would you want your children to have?

4. What kind of values are you teaching your children?

Writing his memoir, <u>Death Dealer: The Memoirs of the SS Kommandant at Auschwitz</u>, Rudolph Höss listed only one regret: "I regret that I did not spend more time with my family." Few people go to their deaths wishing they had spent less time with their children. What are your priorities? What are you doing about them?

Gaining Control of Ourselves

NOTES:

Appendix

Overview of the Workbook

1. What did you like most about this workbook and class?

2. What didn't you like about the workbook or class, if anything?

3. What is the most valuable lesson you've learned?

4. What changes have you seen in yourself?

5. What other topics would you have liked to learn more about?

6. What interesting thing did you learn about yourself that you did not know before?

7. Do you think you have the coping skills to better control your anger and stress?

Selected Bibliography

Anger

Beck, Aaron T., *Prisoners of Hate: The Cognitive Basis of Anger, Hostility, and Violence.* Perennial, 2000.

Ellis, Albert and Raymond Tafrate, *How to Control Your Anger before It Controls You.* Citadel Trade, 1998.

Nhat Hanh, Thich. *Anger: Wisdom for Cooling the Flames.* Riverhead Books, 2002.

Peurifoy, Reneau Z., *Anger: Taming the Beast: A Step-By-Step Program for People With Explosive Anger and Those Who Find It Difficult to Express Anger.* Kodansha International, 2002.

Potter-Efron, Ronald and Patricia Potter-Efron, *Letting Go of Anger: The 10 Most Common Anger Styles and What to Do About Them.* New Harbinger Publications, 1995.

Williams, Redford. *Anger Kills: Seventeen Strategies for Controlling the Hostility That Can Harm Your Health.* Harper Torch, 1998.

Stress

Ali, Majid (M.D.). *What Do Lions Know About Stress?.* Denville, NJ: Life Span Press, 1996.

Charlesworth, Edward A. (Ph.D.) and Ronald G. Nathan (Ph.D.). *Stress Management: A Comprehensive Guide to Wellness.* New York: Atheneum, 1984.

Davidson, Jeff. *The Complete Idiot's Guide to Managing Stress.* Macmillan Publishing Co., Inc., 1996.

Hanson, Peter G. (M.D.). *Stress for Success: How to Make Stress on the Job Work for You.* Doubleday, 1989.

Hawkins, Don. *Overworked: Successfully Managing Stress in the Workplace.* Chicago: Moody Press, 1996.

Herzog, Greg and Craig Masback. *The 15-Minute Executive Stress-Relief Program.* New York: Perigee Books, 1992.

Kiev, Ari (M.D.) and Vera Kohn. *Executive Stress.* New York: AMACOM, 1979.

Leatz, Christine A. (M.S.W.) with Mark W. Stolar (M.D.), *Career Success/Personal Stress: How to Stay Healthy in a High-Stress Environment.* McGraw-Hill, Inc., 1993.

Murphy, Lawrence R. and Theodore F. Schoenborn. (eds.). *Stress Management in Work Settings.* U.S. Department of Health and Human Services, Public Health Service, May, 1987.

Neidhardt, E. Joseph (M.D.); Malcolm S. Weinstein (Ph.D.); Robert R. Conry (Ph.D.). *No-Gimmick Guide to Managing Stress.* Self-Counsel Press, Inc., 1990.

Sehnert, Keith W. (M.D.). *Stress/Unstress: How You Can Control Stress at Home and On the Job.* Minneapolis, Minnesota: Augsburg Publishing House, 1981.

Spera, Stefanie (Ph.D.) and Sandra Lanto (Ph.D.) *Beat Stress with Strength: A Survival Guide for Work and Life.* Indianapolis: Park Avenue Productions, 1997.

Strauss, Sally. *Inner Rhythm.* San Francisco: Chase Publications, 1985.

Yates, Jere E. *Managing Stress.* New York: AMACOM, 1979.

Emotional Intelligence

Goleman, Daniel. *Emotional Intelligence: Why It Can Matter More Than IQ.* Bantam, 1997.

Goleman, Daniel, Annie McKee, and Richard Boyatzis. *Primal Leadership: Realizing the Power of Emotional Intelligence.* Harvard Business School Press, 2002.

Goleman, Daniel. *Working with Emotional Intelligence.* Bantam, 1998.

Hedges, Lawrence E. and Anthony G. Brailow. *Strategic Emotional Involvement.* 1996.

Howell, William Smiley. *Empathic Communicator.* 1981.

Ickes, William. *Empathic Accuracy.* Guilford Press, 1997.

Knapp, Mark L. *Nonverbal Communication in Human Interaction.* Holt, Rinehart & Winston, 1972.

McCarthy, Jim. *Dynamics of Software Development.* Microsoft Press, 1995. (*An excellent application of the principles of emotional intelligence to teamwork in industry.*)

Millman, Dan. *Way of the Peaceful Warrior: A Book that Changes Lives.* H. J. Kramer, 2000.

Omdahl, Becky Lynn. *Cognitive Appraisal, Emotion, and Empathy.* Lawrence Erlbaum Assoc., 1995.

Ruiz, Don Miguel. *The Four Agreements: A Practical Guide to Personal Freedom.* Amber-Allen Publishing, 1997.

Smith, David Woodruff. *The Circle of Acquaintance: Perception, Consciousness, and Empathy.* 1989.

Communication

Faber, Adele and Elaine Mazlish. *How to Talk so Kids will Listen and Listen so Kids will Talk: 20th Anniversary Edition.* Avon, 1999.

Fisher, Roger, William Ury, and Bruce Patton. *Getting to Yes: Negotiating Agreement without Giving In.* Penguin Books, 1991.

Rosenberg, Marshall. *Nonviolent Communication: A Language of Life.* Puddledancer Press, 2003.

Stone, Douglas, *et al. Difficult Conversations: How to Discuss What Matters Most.* Penguin, 2000.

Tannen, Deborah. *You Just don't Understand.* Ballantine, 1991.

NOTES:

Index

A

ABCD · 87, 88, 96, 102
ability · 18, 20, 21, 23, 37, 55, 62, 63, 64, 65, 67, 68, 69, 75, 104
abuse · 23, 63, 82, 85, 97, 122, 123
abused · 18, 122
accept · 37, 44, 45, 46, 104, 106, 110
acceptable · viii, ix
acceptance · 37, 38, 44, 54, 62, 64, 109
accepting · 20
accurate · 104
action · ix, 3, 19, 66, 67, 68, 80, 82, 96, 97, 122
active listening · 6, 110, 111
adapt · 37
addiction · 67
adrenaline · 1, 37, 38, 60
advice · vi, 44, 55, 107, 110
aggression · 1, 3, 18, 20, 22, 23, 39, 59, 63, 81, 97, 99
aggressive · 1, 2, 4, 18, 81, 87, 112, 118
aggressive communicator · 112
aggressively · 1, 39, 84
agitated · 41
agreement · 79, 98
alcohol · x, 85, 98, 99, 122, 123
always · 31, 41, 46, 47, 67, 72, 76, 78, 115, 123
analysis · 110
anchor · vi, vii, 4
anger · i, vi, vii, viii, ix, 1, 4, 16, 17, 18, 19, 20, 21, 22, 23, 36, 39, 40, 63, 64, 66, 72, 75, 76, 77, 78, 79, 80, 81, 82, 84, 87, 88, 89, 91, 94, 95, 96, 97, 99, 100, 102, 112, 126, 127
anger log · 97
anger management · 1, 16, 17, 18, 21
angrily · 21, 87
angry · viii, ix, 1, 16, 18, 19, 21, 22, 39, 41, 75, 76, 77, 78, 80, 81, 82, 84, 87, 88, 91, 95, 96, 98, 99, 102, 108, 111, 113
angry feelings · 1
anxiety · 36, 38, 52, 77, 89
apathy · 40, 82
appraisal · 82
appraise · 63, 82
argue · 100
argument · 41, 99, 100, 118
arousal · 1, 18, 97
assertive · 112
assertive communicator · 112
assertiveness · 6
attention · vii, viii, 21, 42, 49, 55, 79, 80, 108, 109, 122
attitude · 122
authority · 79, 107
automatic · 65, 67
avoidance · 7, 108
aware · ix, 41, 52, 68, 77, 78, 81, 87, 123
awareness · 36, 38, 67, 123

B

bad habits · 67
behavior · ix, 1, 4, 5, 16, 40, 41, 62, 65, 66, 67, 69, 70, 81, 84, 85, 94, 97, 98, 112, 113, 122, 123
behaviors · vi, viii, 5, 56, 65, 82, 84, 85, 100, 122, 123
beliefs · 25, 32, 64, 65, 66, 73, 74, 104
blame · 3, 19, 87, 98, 112
blood pressure · 1, 36, 40, 48, 52, 77, 81
bloodstream · 1, 37, 48, 60
blowing up · 52
body · 1, 18, 36, 37, 40, 42, 43, 47, 48, 49, 52, 60, 63, 65, 68, 76, 82, 99
brain · 47, 63, 65, 66, 69, 75, 76, 78

C

calm · 17, 43, 45, 49, 77, 99
calm down · 17, 45
calmly · 21, 22
cancer · 36, 38, 58
challenge · 37, 69
change · vii, 19, 22, 28, 32, 33, 37, 44, 47, 65, 66, 67, 69, 74, 79, 82, 88, 96, 97, 105, 108, 117
check in · 99, 105
children · ix, 19, 23, 29, 30, 68, 85, 91, 116, 117, 122, 123, 124
choice · 24, 63, 67, 81, 106
choose · 70, 78
clarify · 96
commitment · 46, 79
communicate · 54, 63, 80, 105, 109, 112, 115, 122
communicating · 80, 87, 99, 105, 108, 109, 114
communication · vii, ix, 1, 16, 54, 55, 62, 67, 68, 76, 79, 98, 104, 105, 107, 109, 110, 112, 118, 119, 122, 123, 129
communication techniques · ix
communicator · ix
compassion · 64, 123
compromise · 6, 68, 106, 118
conflict · viii, 16, 22, 54, 65, 66, 68, 80, 112, 114, 118
confrontation · ix
connect · 41, 69, 70, 74, 110
connection · 62, 69, 77, 80
conscience · 69
conscious · 65, 66, 70
consequences · 66, 67, 77, 78, 81, 87
constructive interaction · vii
contempt · 82
contrasting wheels of behavior · *See* Wheels
Contrasting Wheels of Interactions · See Wheels

control · i, viii, ix, 1, 3, 16, 19, 20, 21, 22, 25, 37, 39, 41, 52, 58, 65, 66, 67, 70, 71, 78, 80, 81, 82, 84, 85, 88, 89, 95, 96, 97, 98, 99, 100, 102, 113, 123, 126, 127, 128
control yourself · 70
controlling · 7, 127
conversation · 55, 67
cooperation · 64, 123
cope · 16, 37, 65
coping · ix, 36, 38, 47, 54, 59, 100, 101, 126
coping skills · ix, 126
counseling · 47
coward · 99
creative · 46, 66
crisis · 66
critical · 68
cues · ix, 98

D

damag · 19, 63, 122
damage · 18, 19, 44
danger · 36
decision · 21, 31, 62, 63, 66, 68, 69, 116, 123
de-escalate · 97
demanding · 88, 89
dependent · 68, 73, 74
depressed · 48, 72, 82
depression · viii, 36, 38, 40, 47, 72, 73, 84, 123
destructive · viii, 80, 97
destructive interaction · vii
disagreement · 98, 112
discipline · 117
discontent · viii
discouraged · 72, 73, 80
discussion · 116
disease · 36, 38, 41
disgust · 64
displeasure · 1
dominate · 5
domination · 82
drinking · 17, 40, 48, 99
drugs · x, 85, 98, 99, 116, 122, 123
dysfunctional · 52

E

effective · ix, 21, 54, 55, 68
emotion · viii, 16, 22, 72, 75, 76, 77, 80, 113
emotional · vii, ix, 1, 2, 4, 17, 47, 48, 52, 53, 59, 60, 62, 63, 66, 69, 73, 74, 76, 77, 78, 81, 99, 105, 108, 112, 122, 123, 129
emotional intelligence · vi, vii, ix, 1, 2, 4, 17, 62, 66, 68, 78, 105, 112, 128, 129
emotions · 16, 20, 23, 39, 40, 45, 62, 63, 64, 65, 66, 68, 69, 70, 75, 89
empathic · 69, 110
empathy · 64, 69, 70, 80, 109, 129

empowered · 21
endorphins · 47
energy · 16, 21, 47, 60, 66, 68, 72, 75, 76, 78
evaluation · 68, 107, 109, 110
exaggerating · 44
exercise · 42, 46, 47, 54, 55, 99, 105
exercises · vii, ix, 47
exhaustion · 39, 84
expect · 31, 46
expectation · 73
expectations · vii, 39, 46
experience · 24, 32, 36, 40, 44, 45, 65, 69, 77, 82, 85, 99, 122
explode · 21
explosive · 1, 81, 84, 100
express · viii, 39, 45, 54, 63, 76, 81, 82, 98, 100, 105, 109, 110, 112, 115
expressing anger · ix
expression · viii, 16, 63, 68, 81, 82, 84, 109, 110
eye contact · 112

F

factors · 1, 39, 84, 88
failure · 82
family · ix, 25, 27, 31, 39, 46, 68, 85, 104, 122, 123
fatigue · 36, 39, 84
fear · viii, 44, 45, 64, 66, 72, 77, 99
feedback · 6, 67
feel · ix, 16, 17, 18, 21, 28, 29, 30, 33, 39, 41, 42, 43, 48, 49, 53, 54, 62, 63, 69, 70, 72, 73, 74, 76, 77, 78, 80, 87, 91, 96, 97, 98, 99, 100, 108, 110, 111, 113, 114
feel good · 69, 78
feeling · ix, 1, 19, 21, 36, 39, 49, 52, 54, 70, 72, 73, 76, 77, 81, 82, 85, 86, 87, 95, 98, 105, 109, 110, 111, 113
feelings · viii, ix, 1, 2, 3, 6, 16, 36, 39, 41, 42, 43, 54, 62, 63, 64, 65, 66, 67, 68, 72, 76, 77, 78, 80, 81, 82, 84, 85, 87, 88, 89, 91, 92, 93, 96, 98, 100, 104, 105, 106, 108, 109, 110, 112, 113, 119, 122
fight · 1, 36, 37, 47, 60, 76, 99, 100, 122
flexible · 20
flight · 36, 37, 60
focus · 1, 20, 21, 45, 73, 95
focusing · 4, 6, 43, 108
forgiveness · 64
freeze · 36, 37, 60
friends · 19, 27, 28, 29, 46, 85, 91, 116
frustrate · 20
frustrating · 20, 52, 53
frustration · 1, 20, 21, 52, 82, 89

G

goal · ix, 66, 73, 78, 96, 98
Golden Rule · 69
grateful · 43
grief · 24, 77

growth · 38, 39, 57, 79, 84, 105

H

habit · 4, 67
habits · 32, 56, 69
happiness · 70, 71, 78
harmful · ix, 22, 36, 60, 75, 81, 122
head · 37, 41, 49, 79, 81
headaches · 36
health · vii, 18, 22, 36, 62, 72, 77
healthy · vi, 1, 4, 70, 104
heart · 36, 38, 40, 47, 48, 66, 68, 77, 109
heart attack · 36, 38, 77
heart rate · 36, 77
heartbeat · 49
helpless · 39, 85
high-risk · 39, 59, 84, 100
high-risk factors · 39, 84, 100
hopeless · 39, 73, 85
hostile · 81, 112
hostility · 7, 82, 127
human need · *See* needs
hurt · 18, 63, 69, 82, 104, 113, 115
hurtful · 70, 81, 119

I

I messages · 112
I told you so · 115
identify · viii, ix, 22, 39, 52, 53, 59, 70, 76, 84, 96, 105
ignore · 67
illnesses · 47
immune system · 36, 41
impact · 3, 28, 62
impulsive · 67, 84
impulsively · 21
inappropriate · 16, 20, 39, 63, 66, 80, 84, 85
inattention · 7, 40
ineffective · 1
influence · viii, x, 65, 67, 87, 107, 112
intelligence · vii, 2, 81
intelligent · 22, 63
intense · 18, 19, 23, 41, 63, 76, 77, 97
interaction · vi, 4, 20, 68, 79
interpersonal · vii, viii, 1, 21, 22, 62, 104
interpret · 37, 82
interrupting · 7
intimacy · 79, 105
intimidating · 81, 98
intimidation · 7, 82
irritability · 52

J

journal · 57

joy · 62, 64
judge · 87, 107
judgment · 48, 107, 109, 113
judgmental · 115

L

learned response · viii
lesson · 50, 77, 126
listen · 17, 54, 55, 62, 67, 68, 104, 106, 118, 129
listener · ix, 55, 56, 98, 109, 112
listening · ix, 55, 56, 62, 63, 67, 68, 109, 110
log · i, 58
logic · 63, 107, 110
loneliness · 39, 85
lonely · 62, 72

M

maladaptive · ix
manage · vii, ix, 1, 18, 20, 21, 23, 36, 50, 60, 63, 65, 68, 70, 75, 81
manage anger · 84
manipulation · 7
maturity · 105
meditation · 47, 52, 54
mental · 36, 37, 41, 43, 47
mental snowball · 41, 43
message · 67, 88, 96, 104, 109, 110, 112, 113, 114, 122
mind · 17, 41, 42, 49, 66, 70, 78
miscommunication · 5
misunderstood · 16, 17, 72
mood · ix, 48, 63, 112
motivated · 36, 69
motivation · 69, 72, 122, 123
muscles · 1, 36, 37, 40, 52, 60
music · 26, 48
mutual · 98, 112, 114

N

needs · 6, 43, 48, 62, 63, 65, 68, 70, 77, 79, 106, 109, 112
negative consequences · 1, 70, 81
negative feeling · 72
negative wheel · vii, 5, 7
negotiation · 68, 79, 116, 118
never · 44, 77, 108, 115
non-verbal · 67
non-violent · 87
nurture · 70

O

optimism · 62, 69
optimistic · 74

Option · 78, 96
options · 21, 67, 70, 78, 96
outbursts · ix, 1, 2, 19, 20, 81, 87
outcome · 44, 81, 82
overwhelmed · 39, 43, 63, 86

P

parent · 20, 26, 30, 33, 66, 68, 85, 91, 122, 123, 124
partner · 99, 115
passive communication · 112
passive listening · 109
passive-aggressive · 112
patience · 20, 104
pattern · 5, 19, 66, 67, 81
peace · 49
peaceful · 49
pessimistic · 72, 73
physical · 1, 18, 22, 36, 37, 47, 48, 53, 59, 60, 72, 97, 99
positive · vi, vii, 1, 4, 18, 21, 22, 37, 39, 45, 54, 62, 63, 68, 87, 96, 98, 104, 122, 123
positive outcomes · 62
power · 78
powerful · 38, 66, 75, 80, 109, 122, 123
practice · vi, vii, viii, ix, 32, 45, 49, 52, 53, 55, 62, 66, 67, 68, 70, 78, 91, 98, 99, 114
pressure · 1, 20, 36, 38, 39, 63, 76, 81
prevention · vii, 18, 39, 54, 84
primitive · 76, 77
principle · 77, 129
priority · 69
problem · viii, 1, 17, 18, 22, 32, 37, 46, 47, 55, 62, 77, 80, 81, 84, 85, 86, 96, 99, 104, 107, 108, 110, 111, 123
problematic · 1
protect · 54, 65, 76
psychological · 76
psychotherapy · 47
pulse · 1
put-down · 63

R

rage · viii, 1, 7, 19, 20, 21, 22, 23, 40, 63, 82, 97, 99
reacting · 21
reality · 21, 46
recognize · ix, 1, 37, 40, 41, 47, 52, 63, 68, 69, 70, 72, 81, 84, 98, 100, 113, 122
recondition · viii
redirect · 69
reframe · 96
regret · 21
reinforce · 70
relations · 1, 104
relationship · vii, 1, 4, 5, 16, 18, 19, 20, 21, 56, 62, 67, 73, 79, 80, 81, 85, 104, 110, 118
relax · 46, 48, 49, 52, 98, 99, 100
relaxation · 48, 49, 52, 53, 54

relaxation response · 52
rephrasing · 6, 111
resentful · 73
resentment · 82, 85
resources · 37
respect · 106, 109, 123
response · 1, 36, 37, 41, 48, 54, 55, 60, 63, 65, 76, 77, 78, 82, 97
responsibility · i, ix, 39, 113, 122
rest · 46
revenge · 21
rights · i, 82
roadblocks · 1, 122
role model · 68
role modeling · 70

S

sabotage · 21, 78
safe environment · 53
safety · 62
sarcasm · 82, 108, 112
school · vii, viii, 20, 39, 128
secondary · 72, 75, 76
self-centered · 88
self-control · 70
self-destructive · viii
self-esteem · 40, 82, 112, 122
selfish · 67
self-statement · 45
self-talk · 44, 45, 49, 67, 68, 94
shame · 80, 85
signal · ix, 16, 18, 34, 76, 82, 96, 100, 109
signs · 37, 40, 41, 84, 96
skill · viii, 48, 55, 62, 67, 68, 70, 105
skills · vi, vii, ix, 4, 16, 21, 22, 37, 38, 48, 53, 55, 56, 60, 62, 68, 79, 102, 104, 105, 112
smoking · 17, 48
social · 68
socialization · 68
socialize · 68
society · 22, 63, 80
sorrow · 64
spokes · vii, ix, 4
stimulus · 65, 78
strategies · 39, 54, 59, 65, 66, 84, 100
strength · 47, 80
stress · vii, ix, 1, 16, 17, 18, 36, 37, 38, 39, 40, 41, 43, 44, 45, 46, 47, 48, 49, 50, 52, 53, 54, 57, 58, 60, 63, 72, 77, 80, 81, 85, 102, 126, 127, 128
stress journal · ix
stress management · 1, 37
stressor · 37, 41, 58, 59
stressors · 1, 37, 38, 39, 57
styles of communication · 112
success · 20, 62, 86
support group · 46
surprise · 64
swearing · 82

symptom · 42
symptoms · 36, 37, 40, 41, 42, 43, 53, 60
systematic desensitization · 52

T

technique · 50, 52, 53, 67, 76, 78, 97
techniques · viii, ix, 17, 36, 48, 52, 53, 54, 104
temper · 82
tense · 1, 17, 37, 52, 60
tension · 16, 36, 37, 52, 99
thinking · 41, 55, 67, 70, 72, 87, 88
thought · 39, 41, 42, 49, 64, 67, 68, 75, 87, 88, 91, 96, 97, 109, 114
threat · 36, 37, 39, 63, 84
time management · 39
time-out · ix, 52, 53, 94, 97, 98, 99, 100
traffic · 32, 34, 39, 41
troubled · 1, 85
TV · 17, 25, 27, 48

U

ulcers · 38
unconscious · 69, 70
understand · vii, 62, 64, 65, 67, 72, 75, 81, 87, 104, 110, 111, 115
understanding · ix, 2, 37, 62, 67, 80, 104, 110
unfair · 21
unfairness · 20
unhappiness · viii
unite · 64

unmet · 62, 73, 76
unresolved · 81
upset · 17, 39, 41, 54, 77, 82, 87, 96, 98
upsetting · 41, 45, 88, 96
uptight · 41
utilize · 37, 62

V

venting · 20, 52
verbal · 55, 67, 68, 97, 109
victim · 3, 80
violence · vii, 3, 18, 20, 22, 23, 63, 81, 87, 123, 127
violent · viii, ix, 2, 22, 81, 82, 84, 87, 97
violently · 1
vulnerability · 80
vulnerable · 16, 84

W

well-being · 69
wheels · vi, vii, ix, 4, 6
worried · 44
worries · 44

Y

yoga · 47

Gaining Control of Ourselves

NOTES: